SAṂVĀDA

DIALOGUES ON ONENESS

LIGHT OF VEDANTA PRESS

WITH
SWAMINI SVATMAVIDYANANDA

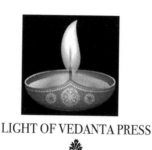

तद्विद्धि प्रणिपातेन परिप्रश्नेन सेवया

Saṃvāda: Dialogues on Oneness

ISBN: 978-1-5136-9738-3

Arsha Vijnana Gurukulam
1190 W 27th Ave, Eugene, OR 97405
For more information visit: https://www.arshavg.org

Pujya Sri Swami Dayanandaji

येन गीर्भिर्निगीर्णो वै तिमिरौघस्समन्ततः ।
महावाक्यमहोल्केन हृदीडेऽहं दयाद्युतिम् ॥

I worship in the heart the great firebrand of the mahāvākya and the beacon of compassion, by whose words the deluge of self-ignorance was indeed swallowed up in its entirety.

Sri Swami Sakshatkrtanandaji

वाटिका गुरुवाक्यस्य यस्यायासेन वर्धिता।
साक्षात्प्रमाणकेदारसमाम्नात्रे नमो नमः॥

Repeated salutations unto the manifest curator of the sacred repository of the knowledge of the self-evident self, by whose efforts the garden of the Guru's words has been greatly augmented.

SWAMI DAYANANDA ASHRAM
(Sri Gangadhareswar Trust)

PREFACE

I am very happy to write a preface for this wonderful book by Swamini Svatmavidyananda. It is a beautiful collection of answers for questions raised at various satsangs by students, brought out with a systematic classification of various topics.

This book will be a very useful tool for spiritual aspirants to look for guidance on particular topics. Swaminiji has very clearly handled various questions, giving comprehensive answers from her direct vision that goes and strikes at the heart of the questioner.

This book can serve as a *prakaraṇa-grantha*, and can be taught as such. I am sure that the book will reach many seekers of self-knowledge and help them understand the intricacies of Vedanta. I wish Swaminiji all success and hope that more books will come from her.

Swami Sakshatkrtananda
Chairman and Managing Trustee Cum Chief Acharya

Swami Dayananda Ashram, Swami Dayananda Nagar, Muni Ki Reti-249137 RISHIKESH, (Tehri Garhwal)
UTTARAKHAND | Phone (0135) 2430769, 2438769
E-mail: dayas1088@gmail.com, Website : www.dayananda.org

Dedication
Srimati Ratna Rao

माता गुरुतरा भूमेः । ।महाभारतम् ३।२९७।४१

The Mother is greater than Mother Earth.

॥*Mahabhārata 3.297.41*॥

arsha vijnana gurukulam

8570 Village Place
Suwanee, GA 30024
(470) 564-0644
arshavg.org

1190 W 27th Ave
Eugene, OR 97405
(541) 684-0322
arshavm.org

FOREWORD

On *Gurupūrṇimā* day, a group of students presented me with the transcription of many question-answer sessions held during several residential retreats at Arsha Vidya Gurukulam, Saylorsburg, PA., Washington D.C. and Sivananda Ashram, Nassau, Bahamas. They desired for it to be published in the form of a book so that it would reach a wider audience. This book is a result of their initiative.

I commend the transcription team for their painstaking work. Kudos to Surekha Bhatt, Veena Bhide, Harinder Khalsa, Meena Krishnan K. Narayanan, Varalakshmi Niranjan, Vidya Ramanathan, Shubha Ravishanker, and Vinaya Saptarshi. To Chris Almond, Prashant Parikh, Pravina Rodrigues and Niyati Shah– who stayed up nights and meticulously helped with the editing, formatting and getting the manuscript to ready for print– I extend my heartfelt thanks.

Many thanks to Rucha Joshi, who can spot a

typo– that no one else can see– from a mile away, and to Renuka Devi, who helped with typing Sanskrit verses and corrected the transliteration. Jahnavi Iyer, the Grammar Queen, read the whole manuscript and gave excellent suggestions.

Joan Rasch and Kovida Das are part of every project in which I am involved. As always, they stepped up to offer their services for designing and printing the book, for which I am very thankful.

I offer special thanks to their graphic artist, Miranda Blystone, for the beautiful cover design.

This book is a celebration of the *guru-śiṣya paramparā,* where sacred dialogues between the sage and the seeker are an inherent component of self-knowledge. I pray that the book is useful to seekers everywhere.

Swamini Svatmavidyananda Saraswati
Swami Dayananda Ashram, Rishikesh, India
September 23rd, 2024.

Key to Transliteration and Pronunciation of Sanskrit Letters

Sanskrit is a highly phonetic language and hence accuracy in articulation of the letters is important. For those unfamiliar with the *Devanāgari* script, the international transliteration is a guide to the proper pronunciation of Sanskrit letters.

अ	*a*	*(but)*
आ	*ā*	*(father)*
इ	*i*	*(it)*
ई	*ī*	*(beat)*
उ	*u*	*(full)*
ऊ	*ū*	*(pool)*
ऋ	*ṛ*	*(rhythm)*
ॠ	*ṝ*	*(marine)*
लृ	*ḷ*	*(revelry)*
ए	*e*	*(play)*
ऐ	*ai*	*(aisle)*
ओ	*o*	*(go)*
औ	*au*	*(loud)*
क	*ka*	*(seek)* 1
ख	*kha*	*(blockhead)**1
ग	*ga*	*(get)* 1
घ	*gha*	*(log hut)**1
ङ	*ṅa*	*(sing)* 1
च	*ca*	*(chunk)* 2
छ	*cha*	*(catch him)**2
ज	*ja*	*(jump)* 2
झ	*jha*	*(hedgehog)**2
ञ	*ña*	*(bunch)* 2
ट	*ṭa*	*(true)**3
ठ	*ṭha*	*(anthill)**3
ड	*ḍa*	*(drum)**3
ढ	*ḍha*	*(godhead)**3
ण	*ṇa*	*(under)**3
त	*ta*	*(path)**4
थ	*tha*	*(thunder)**4
द	*da*	*(that)**4
ध	*dha*	*(breathe)**4
न	*na*	*(nut)**4
प	*pa*	*(put)* 5
फ	*pha*	*(loophole)**5
ब	*ba*	*(bin)* 5
भ	*bha*	*(abhor)**5
म	*ma*	*(much)* 5
य	*ya*	*(loyal)*
र	*ra*	*(red)*
ल	*la*	*(luck)*
व	*va*	*(vase)*
श	*śa*	*(sure)*
ष	*ṣa*	*(shun)*
स	*sa*	*(so)*
ह	*ha*	*(hum)*

ं	*ṁ*	*anusvara*	(nasalisation of preceding vowel)
ः	*ḥ*	*visarga*	(aspiration of preceding vowel)
*			No exact English equivalents for these letters
ऽ	'	*avagraha*	(indicates a dropped vowel - not pronounced)

1.	Guttural	–	Pronounced from throat
2.	Palatal	–	Pronounced from palate
3.	Lingual	–	Pronounced from cerebrum
4.	Dental	–	Pronounced from teeth
5.	Labial	–	Pronounced from lips

The 5th letter of each of the above class – called nasals – are also pronounced nasally.

ABBREVIATIONS

AG: *Avadhūtagītā*
AM: *Advaitamakaranda*
BG: *Bhagavadgītā*
Bh.G: *Bhajagovindam*
DDV: *Dṛgdṛśyaviveka*
IU: *Īśopaniṣad*
KU: *Kaṭhopaniṣad*
MU: *Muṇḍakopaniṣad*
NS: *Nirvāṇaṣaṭkam*
P: *Pañcadaśī*
ṚV: *Ṛgveda*
SV: *Sāmaveda*
TU: *Taittirīya Upanishad*
VC: *Vivekacūḍāmaṇi*
VS: *Vasiṣṭha-Smṛti*

TABLE OF CONTENTS

INTRODUCTION

Oṁ Śrī Gurubhyo Namaḥ

Human birth is a rare and precious opportunity. Unlike animals that are guided by instinct and lack choices, humans possess free will– a unique ability to seek and attain their desired ends. This free will allows us to pursue various goals. The Vedic tradition talks of the fourfold human pursuit, known as *puruṣārtha*: dharma (harmonious living through right action), *artha* (security), *kāma* (pleasure), and *mokṣa* (liberation). The ultimate and highest pursuit in human life is *mokṣa*, which is freedom from a sense of inadequacy, insecurity, unhappiness, fear, and suffering.

Until one gains this freedom, there is an ever-present drive to be more and do more. This desire manifests in the form of various activities and complexes that shape our lives. At a certain stage of maturity, it becomes clear that no matter what we do, acquire, or become, a sense of inadequacy remains. This desperation to feel complete and unbound seems to have no solution, but we feel it must be found somewhere. Responding to this deep yearning, the ancient wisdom of the Upanishads calls out to us in one voice: "Even now, you are the happiness you seek!"

To understand this truth of all, we need a teacher, a guru– a remover (*ru*) of self-ignorance (*gu*). The guru is an embodiment of the fullness we are seeking and is the very agent by which the enigmatic words of the tradition are made to take root in the form of self-knowledge. This "journey" to the self begins with the grace of a proper teacher.

As Gita declares:

> **तद्विद्धि प्रणिपातेन परिप्रश्नेन सेवया।**
> **उपदेक्ष्यन्ति ते ज्ञानं ज्ञानिनस्तत्त्वदर्शिनः ॥**
>
> *tadviddhi praṇipātena paripraśnena sevayā* I
> *upadekṣyanti te jñānaṃ jñāninastattvadarśinaḥ* II
>
> Understand that (knowledge) by prostrating reverentially, through asking proper questions, and through service to the teacher. The wise ones, who have the vision of the truth will teach you this knowledge. II BG 4.34 II

This verse highlights the importance of approaching a proper teacher with heartfelt attitudes of service, inquiry, and the suspension of self-limiting conclusions.

We hope that in this book, you will see an embodiment of the spirit of this verse through the questions and answers that follow. Throughout this offering of knowledge, Swaminiji Svatmavidyananda has demonstrated the art of listening and responding to both the person and the question. In these loving teacher-student dialogues (*saṃvāda*), she takes us on a journey of compassion guided by the timeless Vedic wisdom discovered long ago by our ancient *ṛṣis* and *ṛṣikās*.

These dialogues were offered during camps at Arsha Vidya Gurukulam, Saylorsburg, PA., and at Sivanananda Ashram Yoga Retreat, Nassau, Bahamas. This is a compilation of nine satsangs that took place in these camps. The topics are varied, including all four *puruṣārthas* mentioned above, and the vision of oneness unfolded by Swaminiji.

We sincerely hope this book will help seekers gain more clarity. We pray to *Īśvara* to bless all of us with abundant grace in pursuing self-knowledge and removing all obstacles on this journey.

Students of Swaminiji from
Arsha Vidya Gurukulam, Saylorsburg, Pennsylvania;
Arsha Vijnana Gurukulam, Atlanta, Georgia,
Washington, D.C., and Eugene, Oregon;
Sivananda Ashram Yoga Retreat, Nassau, Bahamas.
September 23, 2024

Chapter 1
SAṂSĀRA

Understanding Saṃsāra

Question: What is *saṃsāra*? Why do you say that it is a catch-kill-eat mentality? Why do we lose ourselves in the catch-kill-eat mentality?

Answer: *Saṃyak sarati iti saṃsāraḥ*. *Saṃsāra* is that which keeps on moving in a seemingly endless loop. The primary elements in the loop are *avidyā,* self-ignorance, *kāma,* unbridled desires, karma, action, and *karmaphala,* result of action. It is easy to see how not knowing one's nature as limitlessly whole and free from all wants, starts a chain of unsavory events powered by one's own discontentment. Due to not knowing the nature of oneself as *pūrṇa*, already fulfilled, one strives for contentment centered on the self by engaging in various actions and taking on numerous pursuits. Regardless of whether the results are in keeping with one's desires or are contrary to them, these results become the impetus for unleashing more actions designed either to improve desirable results or reverse undesirable results. Pujya Swamiji brilliantly described *saṃsāra* as a "life of constant becoming," where people keep striving to "become" something or the other. One is oriented towards becoming well educated, becoming rich, becoming famous, becoming secure.

This incessant *karma-karmaphala* cycle can also be understood as a catch-kill-eat attitude. This mentality is *prākṛta-buddhi*–remnants of bestial instincts from previous lives. Until one pursues Vedanta, everyone has this to a certain extent. An animal has no discipline or self-control when it comes to fulfilling its needs. In the same way, many people think that life is meant for instant gratification. They go to great lengths to gain what they want, unmindful of other's rights and needs.

To break the *saṃsāra* loop one begins by transforming the *prākṛta-buddhi* into *saṃskṛta-buddhi*. *Saṃskṛta-buddhi* is not to be understood as a *buddhi* that knows Sanskrit. Rather, it is a refinement of one's thought and action based on self-discipline and adherence to dharma– to that which is correct, in keeping with universal and local norms, and in keeping with what is right for one to do at a particular stage in one's life.

Without proper introspection or self-enquiry, one falls into the catch-kill-eat mentality because that is what everyone around is doing. Scientists are discovering that a child's brain development is influenced as much by the environment as by genetics. The environment plays a crucial role because the brain is not static; it is constantly growing and responding to external stimuli and ongoing events.

This is why children learn to become frazzled, anxious, and stressed. They see these behaviors rewarded. Anxiety often signifies care and attention, and when children exhibit it, they receive validation. It is not that parents intentionally encourage stress, but anxious children gain a sense of belonging. They feel, "I am like everyone else. I fit in." This occurs partly because there is insufficient reflection happening.

Everyone is caught up in the "catch-kill-eat" race– constantly running, chasing after, and achieving something or the other. If you sit still for two minutes, then something is definitely wrong with you. Even if you do not feel that something is wrong with you, people around you will convince you that something is wrong until you start questioning yourself. When you go on vacation, you must return even more exhausted than when you left. Only then is it considered a proper vacation. These are the unwritten norms influenced by what is currently "trending" in life.

Familial norms also play a salient role, whereby children are rewarded for certain behaviors, like becoming go-getters or overachievers, even if they are not naturally inclined to be that way. In certain families, children are molded into this go-getter mindset. We see many parenting styles that contribute to this. One such style is "helicopter parenting," where parents constantly hover over their children, like a noisy chopper, micromanaging every detail.

Why? Because parents often see their children as extensions of themselves. This is not just an Indian phenomenon, but is also present in Western countries.

For example, when the parents ask the teenager "Are you going out with us dressed like that?" it is clear that the parents see their teenager as an extension of themselves. The parents feel their child reflects them and their values. However, if the neighbor's child dresses in any manner, they are not the least bit concerned, as they do not regard it as their problem. Hence, the term "helicopter parent" describes this over-involvement, as the result of which children become hyper vigilant of their accomplishments in order to solicit parental approval.

Then, of course, there are the typical "tiger moms" and "tiger daddies." What do they do? They praise everyone except their own children. Instead, they are hypercritical because of a strange and unfounded belief that praising their child will "spoil" them. Your child is not a carton of milk that will get spoiled. When the child comes running to the parent and says excitedly "Mom! Dad! I got

99 percent in my exams!" the tiger-parent dourly responds, "What happened to the 1 percent? What were you doing? Where did you go wrong?" This kind of constant criticism leads the child to become an overachiever as a coping mechanism, because that is the only way to gain some validation or, at the very least, to get the parents off one's back, even if the validation is absent. This is the environment in which one grows up. What one sees, one does. Additionally, there is a desperate need to belong and gain social validation. Therefore, when the whole world appears to be moving in a certain direction, people want to follow the same path.

This is evident in how people greet each other. After exchanging names, "What do you do?" is invariably the next question. If you respond, "I do not really do anything," no one can comprehend this answer. "How can you be like that? Are you independently wealthy? Do you have a trust fund? Is there some money coming in?" When you answer "no" to all these questions and insist that you do nothing, it causes shock waves. Suddenly, you find yourself not getting any calls to hang out, with friends or even for a Google Hangout. The *Kaṭhopaniṣad*, recognized this problem a long time ago:

पराञ्चि खानि व्यतृणत्स्वयम्भूस्तस्मात्पराङ्पश्यति नान्तरात्मन्। कश्चिद्धीरः प्रत्यगात्मानमैक्षत् आवृत्तचक्षुरमृतत्वमिच्छन्॥

parāñci khāni vyatṛṇatsvayambhūḥ
tasmātparāṅ paśyati nāntarātman ।
kaściddhīraḥ pratyagātmānam
aikṣatāvṛttacakśuramṛtatvamicchan ॥

By arranging all the sense organs to face the external world, it is as though the Lord has destroyed (the human race). One is, therefore, outwardly focused, and no one introspects about the *ātman*. Rare is the discerning individual who, by desiring immortality, turns the pursuit inward to know the *ātman*.

॥ KU 2.1.1 ॥

Here, Lord Yama provides an ingenious explanation for why everyone is caught in the catch-kill-eat mentality. He suggests that it is not the people's fault at all. "Oh, really?" Then who is to blame? "*Bhagavān*!" I like this; I find that it is very comforting for the *jīva*, the individual, drowning in the deluge of *saṃsāra,* to know that the predicament in which one finds oneself is not one's own fault.

One feels a peculiar relief thinking thus: "*Bhagavān* is to be blamed." Why? Because consider what *Īśvara* has done. If *Īśvara* really wanted us to go inward, our eyes would not face outward, constantly seeking prey. Our ears would not be oriented outward, always searching for sounds to indulge in. We are perpetually mesmerized by sense objects because all our sense organs are directed outwards. It seems as though *Bhagavān* has, in a way, set up the individual for outwardly pursuits, destroying, as it were, any chance of *mokṣa*.

In this scheme of things, it takes a single person of discernment, someone who has carried the yearning for understanding from many lifetimes. Perhaps this person had a glimpse of Vedanta in a previous life and, searching again in this life, decided to defy public opinion. They chose to swim upstream, while the masses swam downstream in the flow of hunting for validation This one individual decided to swim upstream, because it was the right thing to do to get away from this "becoming" mentality and focus on the truth of oneself. It takes one person finally to understand that the self is the truth of everything. How does this happen? Through a revolution of the vision, the inner vision, which is oriented to the vision of no division.

Self-ignorance turns everyone into a validation-
seeker, and an experience-hunter. Not knowing oneself in the vision of the Upanishads as whole, free, and limitless, one mistakes oneself to be an insecure and wanting person. Unable to have self-approval, people seek validation from the entire universe. It is not unusual to ask a complete stranger, "Am I okay?" even though they do not know you at all. This societal madness makes it extremely difficult to escape the catch-kill-eat mentality.

This is why satsang is needed. We seek the company of like-minded people who are also ready to study Vedanta. Even if the thought "I made a terrible mistake by joining this Vedanta retreat" appears, you can just look around and see others pursuing self-knowledge and feel validated for your choices. It is strangely comforting to make a friend over a meal during a Vedanta retreat and realize, "Oh, you live nearby. Wonderful! We should hang out sometime." This kind of friendship is valuable because it supports one in the journey of overcoming self-ignorance. That is why satsang helps and therefore, coming to places of knowledge like ashrams is beneficial for dropping *saṃsāra*.

Chapter 2
RĀGA, DVEṢA, VĀSANĀ

Handling Preferences and Prejudices

Question: Please clarify *rāga, dveṣa, vāsanā,* and *saṃskāra* in terms of their function, location, and effects on the process of "as though" gaining of self-knowledge and enjoying its fruits. Does *ātma-jñānam* also necessarily include the removal of habitual errors?

Answer: Let us start with the last part of the question. For *jñāna-niṣṭhā*, unswerving abidance in self-knowledge, *viparītabhāvana*, habitual orientations, must be eliminated. Habitual orientations are patterns of thought and deeds to which one is accustomed. In other words, one may know oneself as Brahman, yet, out of habit, one may behave like a *jīva,* an alienated individual subject to fear and sorrow. Elimination of these habit patterns can be accomplished through *nididhyāsana*, contemplation on the words of the Upanishads, which one has studied under a teacher. In the beginning, the *jijñāsu*, the student eager for knowledge is like a cow, grazing hungrily in the pastures of the Upanishads. Just as the cow, having had its fill, sits down and chews the cud, so too the student repeatedly recalls the words of the *śāstra,* studied with the guru, and dwells on them. There is a kind of Catch-22 in this situation: until one has a contemplative disposition one cannot contemplate, and until one contemplates, one cannot cultivate a contemplative temperament. To get out of this impasse, one can practice short periods of rumination of the words of the *śruti,* until one becomes naturally contemplative.

Rāga and *dveṣa* refer to strong preferences and prejudices respectively. *Saṃskāra* denotes deep-rooted impressions and behavior patterns, including desires, that have a past. These well-entrenched notions are *saṃskāras*. They are of two types: they can be healthy and beneficial for one's growth, or they can hinder one's spiritual or emotional development.

Vāsanā also means impressions. One of the meanings of this word is "smell." Just as a smell lingers in the air, so too subtle inclinations or tendencies also linger and carry over lifetimes. Like *saṃskāras*, *vāsanās* can be either beneficial or detrimental to one's emotional development.

> **ईश्वरानुग्रहादेव पुंसामद्वैतवासना।**
> **महद्भयपरित्राणाद्विप्राणामुपजायते॥**
>
> ***Īśvarānugrahādeva puṃsāmadvaitavāsanā*** I
> ***mahadbhayaparitrāṇādviprāṇāmupajāyate*** II
>
> By the grace of *Īśvara* alone, the desire for non-duality arises in the wise to protect them from great fear. II AG 1.1 II

This phrase means that for a human being, there is a subtle inclination towards *advaita*, which, like a bloodhound, the person picks up the scent of non-duality in this birth and pursues Vedanta. This is an example of a beneficial *vāsanā*. There can be inimical *vāsanās* that lead to addictions or undesirable behaviors.

Past Lives

Question: I have read and seen on TV that some three or four-year-old kids remember their past lives, *vāsanās*, and details about their towns, husbands, parents, etc. Why are they carrying their old *vāsanās*?

Answer: These children carry the memories of their past life so that the rest of us can appreciate the evidence for rebirth. In a way, they are doing us a favor by providing proof. There was a recent study conducted in Europe on children who remembered their past lives, and interestingly, quite a few of them were chosen from India. This is because the *Veda* believes in rebirth. As we follow the *Veda* with reverence, we do not ridicule or suppress memories from previous lives, and therefore it is not surprising that there are many instances of remembered past lives from India.

A couple of decades ago, I remember reading a story in the newspaper: One day, a small boy, aged three or four years old, said, "I want *pakoras*." His mother offered to make them, but the boy declared, "You are not a very good cook. My wife makes the best *pakoras*!" Amused, the mother asked, "What are you talking about? Where is your 'wife'?" The boy then vividly described his "wife's" home in another town nearby. Intrigued, the parents decided to take him there. Once there, the boy joyfully bounded through the streets, greeting random strangers by name, and accurately identified the house of his past life. Upon entering the house, the child hugged an elderly woman, saying, "This is my wife." He knew all the intimate details of the house, such as where they kept the money, sugar, and flour. They even had *pakoras*, as that is what they had come for. Eventually, both families agreed never to repeat the visit, as it was unsettling for everyone involved. Such stories are not uncommon in India.

As for the future of these kids, they usually forget these memories as they grow. School, peers, and life experiences help them move on. Rarely do these memories persist into adulthood, and even if they do, they become vague over time.

Chapter 3
DHARMA

Dharma and Karma

Question: You spoke about Duryodhana and said that he did not follow dharma. Can you please elaborate on that?

Answer: Duryodhana was an *ātatāyin,* an ancient terrorist. In the English language, we use the term "terrorist" loosely to refer to anyone who endangers the public, but in Sanskrit, the one who can be known as *ātatāyin* must fulfill any or all of these six conditions:

अग्निदो गरदश्चैव शस्त्रपाणिर्धनापहः।
क्षेत्रदाराहरश्चैव षडेते ह्याततायिनः॥

agnido garadaścaiva śastrapāṇirdhanāpahaḥ ।
kṣetradārāharaścaiva ṣaḍete hyātatāyinaḥ ॥

May one know these six as terrorists: an arsonist, a poisoner, one who is impulsive in the use of weapons, a robber of wealth, land, and wife of another. II VS 3.19 II

Duryodhana checked all the boxes. He lured the Pandavas into a house made of wax in the forest and set fire to it. He poisoned Bhima, grabbed the kingdom and wealth of the Pandavas, and also set his sights on Draupadi, the wife of the Pandavas. All this is *adharma.* In those days the *ātatāyin* was punished with a death sentence.

Question: How does one balance living in the world, fulfilling our karma, and fulfilling our desires, while still turning to *bhakti* and Vedanta?

Answer: We keep Vedanta in our lives as the foremost pursuit and then do the other things as a way of qualifying for the study of Vedanta. We perform action for purifying the mind and heart. Pujya Swamiji's inimitable example of going to the airport comes to mind. It is a wonderfully apt example to illustrate the spiritual journey due to the parallels between the airport and *mokṣa*. You go to the airport to take off to a different destination, and similarly, when you choose to pursue *mokṣa*, you take off in your spiritual journey to a different vantage point, from where all overwhelming problems and challenges that one was dealing with become tiny like the roads and buildings seen from the window as the airplane takes off and gains altitude.

Let us say you are going to the airport and along the way, you get a text message that your flight is delayed by a couple of hours. Naturally, you think, "I have so much time, maybe I can stop at a grocery store and pick up something to eat on the plane." When you go to the grocery store, where are you headed? The answer is "airport." You are not buying groceries for the whole week. You do not get distracted. You pick up a snack and come out of the store. You still have time, so you decide to drop off your clothes at the dry cleaners'. When you go to the dry cleaners', where are you headed? Again, the answer is "airport."

Next, you realize you have more time and decide to call a friend who lives near the airport. The friend invites you over for tea, and offers to drop you at the airport. You have accomplished many things on the way to the airport, without losing sight of your destination. Despite doing many things on the way– dropping off dry cleaning, picking up something, visiting a friend, having tea– everything you do is on the way to the airport.

Similarly, everything you do in life is en route to *mokṣa*, freedom from being a wanting person. Education, career, marriage, children are all like stops along the way. No matter what one does or what desires to pursue, one can still be headed for *mokṣa,* as long as there is *puruṣārtha-niścaya,* ascertainment of what one really wants.

What one really wants is the infinite, which is oneself. This means that one clearly sees the limitations of all objects and pursuits in the *jagat*. One understands that all objects are finite and all pursuits are dead-end pursuits. Furthermore, the infinite is never away from oneself. You are already infinite, already free. The nature of the *ātman* is to reveal everything, and therefore it can never be hidden. What is hidden, as it were, is the understanding that you are already what you seek, and therefore you need not pursue anything to be contented; all that you have to do is to drop the ignorance by a committed exposure to Vedanta. This is a tall order, and runs totally contradictory to one's impulses, and to what one sees everyone around oneself doing.

Therefore, the *śruti*, in her infinite compassion, offers two lifestyles in service of *mokṣa*. For those who are ready, there is the monastic lifestyle, marked by the dropping of all pursuits by committing solely to the pursuit of self-knowledge, or, if one is yet to gain readiness, one can pursue the lifestyle of a householder, in which one prepares one's mind to commit to *mokṣa* by gradually gaining emotional maturity and managing one's *rāga-dveṣa*. This is done through the performance of action as sacred duties, and by receiving all results of action reverentially in a spirit of glad acceptance as gifts from the Lord. The Hindu tradition is unique in its total absence of distinction between the sacred and the secular.

Ours is a culture where, starting with one's own body, everything is sacred. Even actions that are considered to be mundane, such as eating, drinking, or bathing are considered sacred. When actions are performed in this way, they contribute to *antaḥkaraṇa-śuddhi,* self-growth through mental purification.

We can illustrate this through understanding the essence of the Hindu marriage. In fact, the ultimate purpose of the Hindu marriage is for both partners to pursue Vedanta together as it can be daunting for one to do it alone. In the Hindu marriage, there is a ritual known as *kāśī-yātrā,* where the groom declares that he is going off to Varanasi, right before the wedding. Varanasi is a sacred pilgrimage site and a place to study Vedanta and Sanskrit. Because it is situated in the North of India, it is a place that is symbolic of *mokṣa*. Many people still believe that if they die in Varanasi they will get *mokṣa*.

For this ritual, the groom faces north, because the northern direction signifies freedom from notions of bondage. He makes a symbolic gesture by taking a few steps in the northern direction, only to be recalled by the parents of the bride, who ask him not to go by himself. They ask the groom to return, to marry their daughter, and take her with him as she too is interested in the pursuit of *mokṣa*. Thus, the institution of marriage, when properly understood, is conducive for emotional growth, which is necessary to pursue *mokṣa*.

In fact, if you are married, you achieve *mokṣa* faster, especially in an Indian marriage, as you have to accommodate not just the spouse, but scores of relatives comprising the extended family. This spirit of acceptance and accommodation, along with the emphasis on duty and service to the society, makes marriage a means to an end, rather than an end in itself. If you take the marriage itself to be the end, then it will surely end.

If you have children, you are again assured of *mokṣa*. They will press every button you never knew you had, especially when they become teenagers. Each time they talk back or argue, it is an opportunity for you to grow. You think that you are raising them, but in fact they are helping you grow to be more patient, more understanding, more accommodative, and more compassionate. Emotional growth is opening the heart to receive the knowledge of Vedanta. Rather than seeking to do something enjoyable, you learn to enjoy whatever it is that you are doing. Nine-tenths of this pursuit is preparation, and one-tenth is knowledge.

Aparigraha, Non-Hoarding

Question: I have a question about *aparigraha*, non-accumulation, especially concerning money.

Answer: Money is Brahman. Money is *Īśvara*. Money is Goddess Lakshmi, You are okay as long as you understand that Goddess Lakshmi belongs to Lord Vishnu, and not to you. However, if you make the mistake of thinking Lakshmi is yours, then she will surely go away. Another thing we should know is that Goddess Lakshmi is a social butterfly. She likes to visit many people and has a large following. One cannot keep her confined to one place. Therefore, the more you give, the more you share her with others, the more she grows. When you do this, she visits you more frequently.

Wealth is given to you; you are not the generator of it. There is no greater delusion than thinking oneself to be a "self-made person." There is no such thing as a self-made man or woman. A person who considers themselves self-made is often the most miserable. The self-made person has a long list of complaints: "I had nothing. I had only two pairs of clothes, one hanging on a tree, the other on my body. One day I had dal and rice to eat, the next day I had rice and dal. There was no electricity in my house, and so I studied under a streetlamp. Then, by the dint of my hard work, I built this entire empire with my bare hands."

If you unpack these statements, you see that everything was already given: two pairs of clothes, given, dal and rice, given, rice and dal, given, streetlight to study under, given, books given, even the brain is given. The self-made man did not make his brain, nor did his mother or father. It was given. It is all given, given, given. If we acknowledge that everything is already given, then there is no authorship or ownership of anything.

Possessiveness is not recommended for a *sādhaka*, a spiritual seeker. You can own many things; it is neither necessary nor practical to give everything away. You can own many things, but what is that you are possessing? More importantly are you the possessor or are you possessed by your belongings? That is the difference between ownership and possession. Ownership is an objective fact. You can say, "My name is on the deed of this house." You can say, "This is my house," and there is nothing wrong with that. But possession is something else. Possession is a dysfunctional relationship between you and the object in question. That is the difference. That is how you make that distinction.

Karma and Conflict

Question: Oṁ Swaminiji, I have a question about karma and conflict. My mother has eight children between the ages of 50 and 60. There is some conflict. I think I understand that there are many karmas at play in my family– the brother-sister karmas and the parent-children karmas. We all have a sense of duty, and my poor mother has to deal with a lot. We siblings fight a lot. There are conflicts each time we get together. How can I rise above this and support my mother in the best way?.

Answer: You are absolutely right. You make a very astute observation that everyone in the birth family has their own karma. There is a certain pecking order, where the children are concerned. There are also well-entrenched conflicts, which start at age 2 and do not resolve even at age 92. There is disharmony, unmet expectations, and discontent. Half the people in the family feel guilty all the time– they keep thinking "Why did I do this? Why did I not do that?" They seem like a perfect match for the other half, who feel hurt all the time.

In this setup, the guilty person keeps on apologizing, and for the hurt person, no matter how much one apologizes, it is never enough. There are many such patterns. It is nice to let go of them. It is not easy, but it is a good idea to disengage a little bit– not in a conflictual way, but softly. Practice a soft disengagement. Allow yourself to be in the space of the *sākṣin*, the observer, and watch.

We practice sitting back and allowing people the space to do whatever they want. Let them quarrel or cry as they need. We are in the place of the observer. When one practices this for sometime, one is no longer threatening to others and becomes safe for all manner of people, some of whom may not even talk to others. This is very beneficial. If you are able to do this, it is the beginning of this kind of disengagement. You are not affected, and when people see that you are in a good place despite what is going on, they will want to know how you are doing it and will want to emulate it themselves.

It is better to set an example because talking about conflict will not achieve anything. Your views might get shot down because, there is a pecking order, and people might not take you seriously. We do this practice for our own self-growth, not to change others, because we fully know that we cannot change other people; we can only change ourselves by understanding that we cannot change others. That is the change we must undergo.

Vākśuddhi
Purity of Speech

Question: How do I cultivate sweet speech?

Answer: There is a Vedic maxim *"satyaṃ brūyāt, priyaṃ brūyāt,"* which means one must speak the truth, but one must also speak it sweetly. You are trying to speak sweetly while remaining truthful. You can say, "There is no need to worry about this," but that is like telling a sad person, "Do not be sad." It does not help. If you tell a person who is worrying, "Do not worry," it also does not help.

Instead, you can say, "Yes, I can see why you are worried. But trust me, in the large scheme of things, it does not matter." You can convey the same message softly, sweetly, and with a smile on your face.

I read an interesting article about communicating with people who have cognitive decline, or some form of dementia, such as Alzheimer's disease. The article said that such people understand what you are saying but cannot handle too much information at once. It overwhelms them. They struggle to process facial expressions and words simultaneously. Apparently, if you frown at them and say, "How many times have I told you not to do this?" or "Don't you see you are repeating yourself?" they might become agitated or even turn violent. They feel they are in danger when someone approaches them with an angry expression. Instead, if you smile brightly and say in a soft voice, "I know you are having a hard day, but you need to eat. Please put that book away and eat your lunch." When you speak kindly, decisively, and calmly, they are more likely to listen and comply.

Caregivers for dementia patients are trained to say everything with a smile, and this approach can help all of us. Try it with your children, your significant other, and everyone else. People are sensitive and look for cues of disapproval on the speaker's face, because they often do not approve of themselves. Look at them approvingly. Talk to them kindly and calmly.

Perhaps this is why Lord Krishna is always smiling. The grieving Arjuna is taught, as though with a smile. Lord Krishna spoke words of wisdom, *prahasanniva*, with a hint of a smile. Lord Krishna is *ānanda svarūpa*, the embodiment of joy. He is a good role model to emulate.

Overcoming Self-Righteousness

Question: I want to know the difference between a righteous person and a self-righteous person. I do certain things, and my kids judge me, saying, "Mom, you are just so

self-righteous." I do not know what they mean.

Answer: A righteous person is one who follows dharma. Although, generally speaking, we do not call someone "righteous," rather, we would say that they are following the righteous path. A self-righteous person, however, is someone who is convinced that others also should follow the path they believe to be right.

A self-righteous person is very unhappy because they expect the world to change according to their whims. When it does not change, they become angry, resentful, or sad. Therefore, it is good to have a sense of humor and allow people to be who they are. If someone comes to you for advice, then it is different because they are asking for guidance. If they do not come to us for advice, but we go around freely distributing advice, it can become a source of conflict and disharmony.

Of course, there are exceptional situations. Suppose you are on the road and see a man beating a child, you can intervene after ensuring it is safe to do so, or you can call the police. If you are a parent, you have the dharma of shaping the values of your offspring. You have to do everything to shape their values. However, at some point, the Indian parent needs to know when to stop parenting. This is true because Indian parents take parenting very seriously and often do not know how or when to stop.

Once an 82-year-old man came to me and said, "My son is not listening to me. Make him listen to me." I asked him, "How old is your son?" He said, "55." That is when I realized that one should stop parenting at 50– not when they turn 50, but when their "child" turns 50!

These are exceptional situations. But in our day-to-day lives, we must recognize that in the world of *Īśvara,* there is a place for everybody. Let them be in their own place and be who they are. "It is not my job to tell them what to do." That is what you have to tell yourself.

Chapter 4
KARMA AND KARMAPHALA

Actions and Fruits of Action

Question: My understanding is that we are all born to exhaust our *karmaphala.* Can you comment on that?

Answer: One is born in a human body to gain this knowledge. As a dog, you can only wag your tail; you cannot gain this knowledge. Only as human beings we can gain this knowledge.

Of course, once you are born, you will exhaust your karma, but only for this life. There is an infinite amount of karma awaiting fructification in a secret bank account known as *"sañcita,"* nicely gathered, which will be the cause of future births as long as one continues to be self-ignorant. If the only purpose of birth was the exhaustion of karma, then one could have been born in any form. Dogs, cats, cows, and tigers are all exhausting karma. As a human being, you can gain this knowledge and, through that, exhaust the self-ignorance, which is the seed-cause for all other lives.

It is said that the human birth is very difficult to attain. We do not realize this, and if we were to know all our previous births, we would be in a state of permanent shock. That is why there is a veil between this birth and other births, so that each time we can start afresh. Trust me, if we knew all our past births, we would be studying Vedanta 24/7, 365 days a year! Therefore, the human being, endowed with free will and uninhibited self-awareness, is the correct *upādhi* for gaining this knowledge.

Other beings are programmed to eat, sleep, and reproduce. They are self-ignorant; the human being is also self-ignorant. What is the difference? Animals only have *ajñāna*, ignorance, but the human being suffers not only from *ajñāna* but also *anyathā-jñāna,* taking oneself to be what one is not, and not taking oneself to be what one is. To put it differently, ignorance of a rope is one thing, but to confuse it for a snake is an entirely different matter. The self, being self-evident, is not totally unknown. Due to self-ignorance, it is mistaken to be as good as the finite body-mind complex. Self-knowledge is primarily the removal of mistaken notions of oneself.

Question: I have concerns about karma. How do you know what is bad or good karma? For instance, some people with cancer might say it is the best thing that ever happened to them, while others might view it as a terrible karma. Similarly, if one's house burns down, some might see it as the worst thing ever, while others might feel relieved of their possessions. How do you distinguish between good and bad karma, or is it just our reaction to it?

Answer: We define bad karma or *pāpa* as uncomfortable situations that one has to face as a result of one's actions not in tandem with dharma. *Pāpa* is something that people generally find distasteful. People cannot handle loss, destruction of property, being robbed, or being defrauded. All these things are considered difficult karma, or *pāpa* because they cause emotional suffering. However, karma does not actually cause emotional suffering– it only causes discomfort. Due to self-ignorance, one converts discomfort into emotional suffering. This conversion is optional, even though it may not seem so. We have the choice, as you mentioned, to see that something positive may come from it.

Typically, when people undergo difficulties, they will be rattled, afflicted by fear or sorrow. Rare is the person who can take things in stride. In the late sixties, Pujya Swamiji's little hut in Rishikesh burned down. He was making tea with a stove when a gust of wind came through. After all, it was just a thatched hut, and therefore it quickly caught fire. He had started writing a commentary on the *Brahmasūtras*, but, alas, everything went up in flames.

This was a time when there were no Google Drives or Cloud storage. On that hot day, there was not a single cloud in the sky either, and the hut burned down quickly. People who had gathered there tried to douse the fire, but the wind was too strong, so everything burned down. Pujya Swamiji accepted it, saying that it was all meant to go. Very few people are like that. Generally, people get agitated and feel victimized by karma. They take it personally.

Reading about the inspiring lives of saints such as Pujya Swamiji can also be helpful in modulating one's reactions to situations. True enough, things never go as planned, and one has to face unexpected losses and challenges. After a period of grieving, one can put the loss into perspective or learn something from it. We can have the *śraddhā,* trust, that everything will be alright, and that we will be shown the way. This means that surrendering to *Bhagavān* as *karmaphaladātṛ,* the giver of the fruits of action, can help overcome emotional anguish.

Question: You had said before that children are born to exhaust their own karma and have their own karmic trajectory. But their actions also affect us. Does the child's karma affect my karma and cause me to suffer? That has certainly been and continues to be my

experience? Why do I feel affected by the karma of the children?

Answer: This feeling is due to a wrong identification. This identification is expressed in the *śāstra* thus: *putre naśṭe, ahaṃ naśṭaḥ*– if my child is in hot water, I too am ruined, *putre puṣṭe, ahaṃ puṣṭaḥ*, if my child is happy, I too am doing well. You can love your children and be there for them. You can give options, and if they are suffering, you need not suffer along with them. You are more useful to them as a loving observer. By not identifying with their pain, and being free, you will be able to help them come out of it quicker. On the contrary, if you were to say, "Oh no, something terrible happened to you. I am so upset," they will feel doubly burdened. Already they are facing some difficulty, and on top of that, they also have to deal with your feelings about it. This kind of "help" does not really give solace. In fact, it can make them even more agitated.

What gives comfort to the loved ones facing challenges is a caring, but dispassionate response. It is imperative that we practice *asaṅgatva,* non-involvement. *Asaṅgatva* must not be confused with aloofness. It does not mean you do not care; it means that even though you care, you can be in a neutral place and have perspective. Being affected by the offspring's woes is not a symbol of love, rather, it is a sign of codependency and enmeshment in the relationship.

Question: I have a family member who has had a lot of problems in his life. He is always feeling cursed. He feels that the wold is out to get him. He keeps complaining and is depressed. How can I help him?

Answer: This person should start a gratitude journal right away. These days, medical professionals are also recommending this practice. Even if everything seems to go wrong in a person's life, there will always be a few things that one can appreciate. Tell this family member to appreciate at least five things every day. Write five things down, and it is not enough to appreciate them fleetingly. He must write them down and contemplate upon them. He can make this a regular practice. This helps to cultivate an attitude of Everyone feels entitled, thinking, "I should get this. I should have that. Everyone should respect me. Why aren't I getting this respect? Why is this other person getting all the importance?" Such feelings come from the *ahaṅkāra*, the ego. One is not really being targeted but perceives one's life as such.

You cannot tell the person all this directly; perhaps he is not ready to hear it. Feelings of victimization stem from a fear of decimation. Such people are afraid that they will not matter anymore, so they tend to dramatize their life situation and challenges in order to feel noticed and be relevant in others' lives. By encouraging them to write in their gratitude journal every day, you can help them to live more objectively. Expressions of gratitude helps one to emerge from the shell of solipsism. This is a form of *antaraṅga-sādhana*, an inward practice of contemplating upon all that one has been given and reaffirming their interconnectedness to the *jagat* and to *Īśvara*.

There is another exercise that one can do. If the person lives with other family members, you can suggest that for half a day every week, for about four hours, he should not criticize anyone. There should be zero criticism, and only appreciation of people, things, events, and situations. Every criticism should be converted into an appreciation. This practice helps people to change their orientation towards life. This kind of *vāktapas,* disciplined speech can be a *bahiraṅga-sādhana*, an outward practice.

In reality, one is an appreciative, non-demanding, and contented person. That is the truth of who you are. If you start living that truth, it becomes more and more real.

Puṇya and Pāpa

Question: How can I make my *puṇya* grow?

Answer: Actions such as *sevā*, offering service to others, charity, rituals, and prayer make the *puṇya* grow. Listening to Vedanta, teaching Vedanta also makes the *puṇya* grow. In fact, listening to Vedanta is the best way of augmenting *puṇya*.

Question: If *mokṣa* is the goal of life, how do we acquire it? Do we need to spend time acquiring *puṇya* in order to have *mokṣa*?

Answer: The pursuit of *mokṣa* is often not well understood. *Mokṣa* is not the same as going to Starbucks and getting a Mocha. *Mokṣa* is not one more thing to acquire in life. In fact, *mokṣa* is the acquisition of that which is already acquired. *Mokṣa* is one's *svarūpa*, one's intrinsic nature. This nature as free and unfettered by sorrow and fear is eclipsed by wrong notions that need shedding. That is why I say that the word Upanishad should be understood as "upaṇi-shed" because it makes you shed mistaken notions and wrong beliefs about yourself, the universe, and God. When all misidentifications and incorrect notions are shed, what remains is the self-evident self that happens to be infinite. Identifying with this self is *mokṣa*. It is accomplished through a committed pursuit of the study of the Upanishads under a qualified teacher.

In every pursuit, there are karmic obstacles. *Mokṣa* is no exception. These obstacles need to be neutralized so that one can continue on the path until the teachings are well assimilated. Sometimes the mind itself is a powerful obstacle. Coming under its sway, one can stray away from the teachings as one gets attracted to quick fixes and short term fancies.

I will not say that one has to "gather *puṇya* to gain *mokṣa*." Rather, one has to neutralize the *pāpa* standing in one's account. Therefore, in our tradition every ritual begins with a prayer of intent: *mamopātta duritakṣayadvāra srī parameśvaraprityartham idam kariṣye,* which means "I am performing this ritual to neutralize the *pāpa* earned by me and to gain the grace of the Lord. Gathering *puṇya* is not the goal. Ultimately, one recognizes oneself as totally free

of both *puṇya* and *pāpa*. Having great amounts of *puṇya* is a golden shackle, but a shackle nonetheless– it can become an impediment to gaining self-knowledge.

Therefore, it is safer to pray for the *pāpa*– manifesting as obstacles to the study– to be gone. Prayer itself gives *puṇya*. Listening to

Vedanta is *puṇya*. It is not so much about *puṇya* as it is about being prayerful. This helps to ensure that one is not hijacked from this path by the worst of one's own tendencies. In the *Sāmaveda*, there is a very nice *śāntimantra*.

> **माऽहं ब्रह्म निराकुर्यां मा मा ब्रह्म**
> **निराकरोदनिराकरणमस्त्वनिराकरणं मेऽस्तु ॥**
> ***mā'ham brahma nirākuryāṃ mā mā brahma***
> ***nirākarod anirakaraṇam astvanirakaraṇaṃ***
> ***me'stu*** **॥**
>
> May I never deny Brahman; may Brahman never reject me. Let there be no denial; let there be no rejection for me.
>
> ॥ *SV śāntimantra* ॥

The student prays "May I never be in the place where I negate *Īśvara*." This means, may I never say, "you– *Īśvara*– do not exist," or "You are not worth pursuing as the truth of myself." May I never ever see that day. In the second line, the first "*mā*" means "may not," and the second "*mā*" is *mām, which* means "me". This means, may *Īśvara* never reject me. May I never reject *Bhagavān*, and may *Īśvara,* Brahman, never reject me. Let there be non-negation on all sides and let there be non-negation for me. This is a very powerful prayer.

Why would anyone reject Brahman? Denying the existence of Brahman is tantamount to denying oneself says the *Taittirīyopaniṣad: asanneva sa bhavati, asadbrahmeti veda cet.* The one who says Brahman is non-existent is as good as non-existent. Rejection, here, implies being hijacked by strong desires or ending up on a path of self-sabotage. This is the problem. This is how rejection, "as though" rejection, can happen. Why would *Bhagavān* reject you? *Bhagavān* will not reject you at all, but this is *prātibhāsika*, a subjective perception. "God has abandoned me! God does not care!" That is a perception. *Bhagavān* does not reject, because everything is non-separate from *Bhagavān*.

When there is a challenging situation, people immediately assume that *Bhagavān* has abandoned them. This is not true. Sometimes there are difficult karmas that have to be overcome.

You can even say this prayer in English. If you do not remember the Sanskrit, it does not matter. When we say this all the time, the obstacles to the desire for freedom and the desire for knowledge will recede. The fire, the desire for knowledge, will be kept burning brightly, which is what we want.

Chapter 5
ADHYĀSA
Erroneous Perception

Question: How did we gain this wrongful identification with the body and the mind, taking it as "I" instead of just "my body"? Is it from a past birth?

Answer: When something is only partially known it becomes a locus of error. The stock example we have is the rope-snake illusion. Imagine a rope lying on the ground. When is it mistaken for a snake? You cannot project a snake onto an unseen rope or an unknown rope. Similarly, a snake cannot be projected on something that is already known as a rope. When you clearly see it as a rope, you cannot mistake it for a snake. So, when does the snake appear? You can only see the snake on the rope under a specific condition. It happens at twilight, when the rope is only partially visible. You know that there is something on the ground, but you do not know what it is. Only a partially visible rope can be mistaken for a snake.

Just as a half-known rope lends itself to being mistaken for a snake, so too, a partially known "I" leads one to have wrong conclusions about the self. I know that I am, "*ahamasmi.*" I can never say "I am not." Because the self is self-existent, I can never deny my own existence. However, when you ask, "What are you?" or "Who are you?" all my troubles, arising from the mistaken notion that I am finite, bubble to the surface from the depths of the subconscious mind. Thoughts such as "I am not tall enough, I am not strong enough, I am not educated enough, I am not rich enough," come up. Therefore when the *adhyāsa*, erroneous perceptions and identifications centered on the self, resolve, the *adhiṣṭhāna*, the truth of the self, *saccidānanda,* as sentient, limitless existence is known.

Saccidānanda

Question: My question is about self and *saccidānanda*. If the self is already complete, why do I feel a separation from God?

Answer: One is non-separate from everything in the universe but one perceives oneself to be separated. Due to self-ignorance, there is a perception of alienation. For example, in low light conditions, you might look out of your window and see a menacing-looking man standing by the trees. When you shine a flashlight on the "man," he promptly turns into a harmless tree-stump. There is a similar misapprehension with regard to the self.

Likewise, the belief "I am separated from God" is a misperception. When we buy into this misperception, it becomes a burden and feels real, although it is not. The root cause is self-ignorance, because of which I become vulnerable to all kinds of wrong perceptions. "I am" is known, but the knowledge "I am *saccidānanda,*" is not yet fully assimilated. Therefore, thoughts like "I am an idiot" "I am useless" "I am helpless" or "I am no good," arise. Once such thoughts take root, they lead to a feeling of separation from all that is here, including *Īśvara*, God. This misperception can only be corrected by studying Vedanta.

Mithyā and Satya

Question: What is *mithyā?* What is *satya*? How do we remain unswayed by *mithyā* in life?

Answer: The word *mithyā* does not refer to an object; on the contrary, it is a statement about reality. In the tradition, we have the word "*sat*" or "*satya*" which means that which is real. That which is real cannot be negated and is not subject to time.

We have the word *anṛta* or *tuccha* to describe things that are non-existent. The stock example used here is *śaśaśṛṅga,* the horns of a rabbit, which do not exist.

If we take the example of a pot, is it *satya* or *tuccha*? We can see that it does not fulfill the definitions of *sat,* because it is not independent of clay, and because it is subject to time. Yesterday, it was a pot, but then today I accidentally dropped it; therefore, now it has become a "crackpot".

At the same time, we cannot call the pot *tuccha* or non-existent. Why not? Because this pot is available for objectification by the eyes, and serves a particular purpose– in this case, as a teaching-pot, a Vedanta teaching tool.

We do not have a word in common parlance for something that is neither existent nor non-existent. For that, we have to come to Vedanta, which has a special word, *mithyā*. One definition of *mithyā* is that it is *sadasadbhyām anirvācya*– it is neither sat nor *asat*. You can neither say the pot existent, nor dismiss it as non-existent. The first definition of *mithyā* is that whose existence can neither be categorically affirmed nor denied. We see that the pot fulfills this condition.

Our pot is *mithyā* because it also fulfills another definition of *mithyā*– it is *adhiṣṭhāna-ananyat*– non-separate from its source, its cause, namely clay, which is its *adhiṣṭhāna*, its truth, its basis. Wherever there is pot, there has to be clay. The clay pot can never be away from clay.

When we look around, we find that– without exception– all objects in the universe, starting with the body-mind-sense complex, are *mithyā*. *Mithyā* body, *mithyā* mind, *mithyā jagat*, *mithyā* problems and *mithyā* solutions. Then what is *sat*? Where is *sat*? *Sat* is unnegated and self-evident; it is self-existent. *Sat* is you. The one who says, "All this is *mithyā*" is *sadātma*, you. The one who is asking, "What is *sat*?" is you. *Sat* is limitless existence and limitless sentience. This is what we term as *saccidānanda, or satyam-jnānam-anantam*. Other than you, nothing else can be called *sat*. As awareness free of all attributes, you alone fulfill the definitions of *sat* as being unnegated and not subject to time.

When we know *mithyātva*, the *mithyā*-ness of everything, the *jagat* is no longer a source of fear or sorrow. On the contrary, when *mithyā* is mistaken for *sat*, *saṃsāra* descends on one like a personal raincloud that will just not go away. Under its gloomy spell, one becomes *saṃsārified*; one becomes a *samsārin*, subject to sorrow and strife.

Emerging from the hold of *saṃsāra* means emerging from the erroneous perception of mistaking the finite for the infinite. It is a drastic change in one's self-definition– from thinking of oneself as a finite and changing entity, one is established in the knowledge of oneself as the *adhiṣṭhāna,* the source of everything. Being unswayed by *mithyā* requires the committed pursuit of Vedanta. When this pursuit is taken seriously, erroneous perceptions of oneself, the *jagat*, and of *Īśvara* slough off like old skin.

Question: We talked about how we cannot know the *ātman* through the senses, the mind, or by logical inference. I am wondering how that reconciles or compares with the *neti-neti* methodology of negating *anātman* to know the *ātman*.

Answer: First, let us understand what *neti-neti* means. It is, *"na iti", "na iti,"* it is "not this, not this." It is a salient pedagogical tool to remove the mixup between the "I" and the "not-I". Adi Shankara talks about this mixup in the introductory *bhāṣya*, commentary, to the *Brahmasūtra*. He explains that although the *ātman* is free of the body, the mind, or the senses, it gets as-though mixed-up with *anātman*, with the not-I. There is rampant confusion regarding the *paramārthika* "I," the "I" that is consciousness, awareness, which is mistaken for the body-mind-complex due to self-ignorance.

The *neti-neti* pedagogy is a methodology of strategic negation, designed to disentangle the "I" from erroneous identifications. This pedagogy helps us focus on that which remains after everything that does not belong has been negated– namely, the self-revealing *ātman*, which cannot be objectified, and which is free of all attributes.

We have to understand that this negation is a one-way operation. There is nothing in the entire universe that can have its being without the *ātman*, but the *ātman* is independent of everything. The pot cannot be independent of clay, but the clay is free of being pot. It lends its presence to the whole *jagat* of earthenware, without becoming any one object. In the same manner, the body cannot be without the *ātman*, the mind cannot be without *ātman*, the senses cannot be without the *ātman,* but the *ātman* is free of all of them. Here, we encounter a seeming paradox. The body is *ātman*, yet *ātman* is not the body. The mind is *ātman*, but *ātman* is not the mind. The senses are *ātman*, but *ātman* is not the senses. It is a one-way relationship. Due to this confusion, the process of separation is necessary.

We need the methodology of negation and we also need the methodology of affirmation. This method is prominently used in the Upanishads and is also clearly evident in the second chapter of the Bhagavad-Gita:

> **अच्छेद्योऽयमदाह्योऽयमक्लेद्योऽशोष्य एव च।**
> **नित्यः सर्वगतः स्थाणुरचलोऽयं सनातनः ॥**
> *acchhedyo'yamadāhyo'yam akledyo'śoṣya eva ca*
> *Inityaḥ sarvagataḥ sthāṇuracalo'yaṃ sanātanaḥ* II
>
> This (*ātman*) is not subject to being cut or burned, not subject to water-damage or dehydration. It is eternal, all pervasive, and changeless, unmoving, and ever-present. II BG 2.24 II

As we can see, every word in the first line has a negative particle. For instance, *chedya* is something that can be cut. By adding the negative particle "*a*," it becomes *acchedya*, meaning that which cannot be cut. In the same way, we have *adāhya*, not subject to being burnt by fire; *akledya*, not subject to water damage, *aśōṣya*, not subject to air damage. Each negative word here illustrates what *ātman* is not.

Everything in this universe is subject to being destroyed by the five elements. Things decay and succumb to the elements all the time. That is why museums have to work diligently to protect ancient sculptures and paintings. The curators must keep applying protective layers to ensure preservation. Similarly, manuscripts must be coated with protectants to save them from "attaining oneness" with termites. Such preservation efforts are always a race against time because everything is subject to destruction.

The use of the *neti-neti* methodology reveals that the *ātman* is not subject to the five elements. Why? Because the *mithyā* five elements have their being in the *satya-ātman* This is the *neti-neti* methodology in action: understanding that *ātman* is not affected by the five elements, nor is it subject to destruction by any means whatsoever.

Here, a doubt can arise. Since we do not know of anything that exists which is not subject to damage, perhaps the *ātman* is non-existent? This seems like an easy conclusion. Therefore, words like *nitya sarvagata sthāṇu, sanātana* in the next line of the verse provide clarity. *Nitya* means the *ātman* is eternal, always the same, unchanging in every situation– this is a positive affirmation, *"Iti Iti Iti."* *Sarvagata* means it is all-pervasive, not confined to any particular form. *Sthāṇu* means it does not move; it is stationary and unchanging. Together, these methodologies– of negation and affirmation– provide a comprehensive understanding of the *ātman*.

Chapter 6
PRAYER

Surrender

Question: There are different ways to look at prayers. I pray to achieve a certain outcome or result. I pray for wisdom to see the good in all. I pray for strength to endure the storm and reach the other side. Could you explain this a little bit?

Answer: There are many kinds of prayers and many kinds of devotees. Lord Krishna talks about four types of devotees. One type, as you mentioned, prays for a specific outcome, but only in an emergency. This is the "911 devotee"– the emergency number devotee. In every religion, we find such devotees. For them, God is like a 911 service – when all else fails, they have God on speed dial and expect to get immediate help.

The second type of devotee is the one who prays for a specific outcome, often making deals with *Bhagavān*. In India, this is quite common. For example, parents will visit temples just before their children's exams and pray, "O Goddess, help my child pass the exam, and I will give you a nice saree." Is the Goddess waiting for a saree? No, but this is how we pray, and it is an accepted form of devotion. This is the deal-making devotee.

Another example of this type of devotion is from the richest temple in India, the Tirupati Balaji Temple, which netted $94 million last year. Many people love praying to incarnations of Vishnu because he keeps things going, which is what everyone wants. Business owners will name their enterprises "Balaji Enterprises" and ask Lord Vishnu to be the sleeping partner. If the business is successful, they promise to donate 50% of the profit to the temple. Lord Vishnu and his consort Goddess Lakshmi might be highly amused by the thought of them being "sleeping partners," in the business, but it is how many people express their devotion.

Then there is the third kind of devotee, the one who does not seek a specific outcome or keep God on speed dial but instead wants to understand. They ask, "Who are you? Why am I so attracted to you? Show me your form, your name, and show me how you are non-separate from me." This is the *jijñāsu*, the seeker of knowledge.

Finally, there is the fourth type, the *jñānin*, the one who knows he or she is non-separate from God. This person is still a devotee because, as long as the body-mind-sense complex exists, from the individual standpoint, one is a devotee, related to *Bhagavān*. From the standpoint of knowledge, it is all one, and this devotee says, "I am nothing but you."

We tend to ridicule first two types of devotees, dismissing them as ignorant or avaricious. We might consider the second type worse than the first for offering what appear to be bribes to *Bhagavān*. However, Lord Krishna says in the Bhagavad-Gita that all of them are exalted, *udārāḥ sarva eva te*.

The *bhaktās* are all exalted because they have expressed devotion and have taken refuge in the Lord. For instance, the "911 devotee" instead of resorting to crime out of a sense of desperation, chooses to pray. Therefore, they are all exalted.

The idea is to evolve into the third kind of devotee, the one who prays to understand *Bhagavān*, and see *Bhagavān* everywhere. Seeing the good in everything is seeing *Bhagavān* in everything. This is *mokṣa*, freedom, liberation. We say all that is here is God. That is why we transcend the concept of one God, two Gods, or many Gods– because everything is God. When you can appreciate that, there is great maturity. That is self-knowledge. If everything is God, oneself is included in everything.

Overcoming Obstacles

Question: One of the things I want to know is how to overcome obstacles with prayer. I have been staying in the ashram for a few months, but I am now returning to my house.

Can you please give me some direction on how I can continue to stay prayerful and maintain the ashram lifestyle even after leaving the ashram?

Answer: When there is an obstacle, we have to ask, who is the one that puts the obstacle? We can say karma, and karma is another name for *Bhagavān, Īśvara,* God. We can invoke the Lord in the form of *Gaṇapati* or any form you want, and pray, "Please take away these obstacles that are coming in my way." The obstacles could be outer obstacles, like having a goal and encountering blocks that come in the way of accomplishing that goal, or the obstacles could be inner obstacles in the form of hopelessness or lack of self-confidence.

For both inner and outer obstacles, prayer helps. Prayer is karma, action. By initiating new karma in the form of surrender, I inoculate myself against the karmic effects of previous karma. Every karma has twofold results, *dṛṣṭa* and *adṛṣṭa,* immediate results and results that fructify in time. The karma of prayer involves worship and surrender. It creates new *adṛṣṭa* which combats and neutralizes the effect of the old *adṛṣṭa*, from previous lives. It is exactly like getting the Covid vaccine. The vaccine mitigates your chances of getting the virus, but it is not a one shot deal. You have to keep getting booster after booster. I heard of one man who received 147 Covid vaccines in the span of two years. He did this by traveling to various countries and getting vaccinated frequently. Now his body has become a science project, and various studies are being conducted on him.

In the same manner, we keep praying to tackle various *prārabdha*-based obstacles that keep manifesting. This is the best way to deal with the roadblocks of life.

The other thing that you asked is how to have an ashram lifestyle when one is not in the ashram. It is a very important question. It is very difficult, primarily because no one else around you is following the lifestyle. Nobody else is getting up at four o'clock and, after a couple of days, one feels unmotivated to do so. It is difficult to reproduce a schedule designed for collective spiritual living, when one is living away from that environment.

We have learned some important lessons from coronavirus pandemic. Humanity was forced to live, more or less, for nearly a year in isolation. It was continuous and relentless. The pandemic totally reordered the ways in which we live. For three years straight, the contact with people was
severely restricted. It was like an ashram-esque life because there was no other life possible. People who always liked to eat out had to learn to cook. People who were extroverts and could not be without their friends were forced to learn to be at home with themselves. It transformed us. I think *Bhagavān,* in all his *karuṇā*, gave us this virus to reset our spiritual trajectory, and give us an opportunity to reconnect with ourselves. That is why I call it the *karuṇa*-virus.

The other thing about having an ashram-like life outside the ashram is to acknowledge that one's house is not an ashram and that one cannot replicate it exactly without first gaining an appropriate mindset and developing *vairāgya*, dispassion. Until that happens, one has to accept this fact and become gentler with oneself. Otherwise, one soon becomes disappointed with oneself.

At first, one feels bad that one does not have the ashram life; next, one feels bad about not being able to replicate the ashram life in one's home; and finally, one feels bad about feeling bad about oneself. There is a lot of self-flagellation, and inability to forgive oneself for the slightest mistake. For any program of self-discipline to lead to emotional maturity, such discipline must be accompanied by *kṣānti,* accommodation flexibility, and *mārdava*, softness.

The ashram life works because it is gentle. I would encourage you to be soft, and to do everything to discover that you are naturally free of tension. Relax the face, the jaws, the tongue, and the forehead. Tell yourself that there is nowhere to go, nothing to gain, nothing to lose. Tell yourself this every day. Set small and achievable spiritual goals.

If I say to myself, I am going to spend the entire day in meditation, it is a setup for failure, but if I tell myself I am going to practice one-minute-meditation, then I have nothing to lose. For one minute, I can do anything. I can say *"Oṁ namaḥ śivāya"* for one minute without getting distracted or bring the mind back even after getting distracted. This is great. This is wonderful. So, this is what we do. We progress bit by bit, little by little, and be very gentle and compassionate with ourselves. When we do that, we radiate this wellness to the entire world.

Praying Effectively

Question: I was raised in the Episcopal Church, but I have been studying Vedanta also. My question is really about prayer itself. What does it need to be? Some people pray in a temple, some in a church, and some under the stars. Does it have to be a formal "Dear Mary, full of grace!" or can it be something you abstractly ruminate about?

Answer: Prayer can have many forms. While driving you can pray, "Hail Mary, full of grace, please find me a parking space," and if your karma does not interfere, she certainly will.

You can pray in a church, there is no problem with that. You can pray in the form of an elaborate ritual, like a Catholic mass. Or you can pray at home in a *yajña*, a fire ritual. All forms of prayer are valid. God knows all languages, so you do not have to pray in a particular language.

People think, "Oh! If I do not know Sanskrit, I cannot pray." Sometimes, people think prayer means worshiping and adoring God. I need to say a few words about this because sometimes one does not at all feel like adoring God. Why? Often, life is difficult, and one does not like what the difficulties one has to undergo. If God is responsible for everything, and you are having a hard time relating to God, what do you do? In the Hindu tradition, there is a lot of room to express frustration with *Bhagavān* and elevate it to the level of prayer.

You can say to *Bhagavān*, "Are you blind? Are you not seeing what all is happening in my life? How could you do this to me?" and, because of the sincerity in the sentiments, it gets sanctified into a prayer. You cannot scold a non-existent person. You can only complain to someone who exists. Therefore, if you are expressing frustration to *Bhagavān* and using all the choicest words directed at *Bhagavān*, in our tradition, it is not blasphemy; it is a form of prayer. You have made this relationship real. When you take that freedom with *Bhagavān*, it truly becomes a transformative prayer.

In our tradition, we have different forms of devotion, different ways of relating to *Īśvara,* all based on the *iṣṭadevatā* concept. You are free to invoke *Bhagavān* through any form that is pleasing to you, through any form that you find easy to relate to. You can say *Bhagavān* is baby Krishna. Many people relate to Krishna as their child, so we have what is called motherly devotion. Or you can say Krishna is my father. You can say, "I am the baby and Krishna is my father, and the goddess is my mother." That is what we say at the end of the *ārati*: "You alone are the mother; you alone are the father. You alone are the friend."

Mirabai, the famous saint poetess of the 14th century in India, looked upon Lord Krishna as her husband. There are many forms that devotion can take. What is important is that the relationship must be real. It must be enacted, and when that relationship becomes real the heart blossoms and one is transformed. Even if you say many prayers but the mind is elsewhere, it is ineffective.

Saint Kabir said in a couplet:

> **माला तो कर में फिरे जीभ फिरे मुहमाही।**
> **मनुआ तो दस दिसि फिरे यह तो सुमिरन नाही॥**
> ***mālā to kar me phire jībh phire muhamāhī |***
> ***manuā to das disi phire yaha to sumiran nāhī ||***
>
> The beads in the hand go round and round, the tongue in the mouth goes round and round, and the thoughts in the head go round and round. This is not meditation.

This is not prayer. It is just a robotic act. If one thinks that one is supposed to do 10 rounds of *the mālā* and does it distractedly, it is not as effective as just talking to *Bhagavān* sincerely. You have to be authentic, and do whatever it takes to be in sincere communion. To be authentic is to make the relationship real. When this happens, there is an inner transformation.

That is why we have a few steps in the prayer so that it can proceed systematically. In an elaborate *pūjā,* we take the time to sanctify the items used in worship. We also sanctify our bodies and minds and see them as abodes of various deities. The daily *pūjā* need not be very elaborate– it can be just three steps, or five steps if you have a little more time during the week, and occasionally, you can also do a sixteen-step *pūjā*. At the very minimum, you put a little bit of water, some dry fruits at the altar and wave a lamp. You might pray, "May my day be free of obstacles" or "Give me the strength to face whatever comes." But then, let us say, one day you have an important meeting to go to, and you forget to offer to God.

You run out of the house, get into the car, and only then remember, as you start driving off. You were already late to begin with, still, you turn back, get out of the car thinking that you should not leave *Bhagavān* hungry, and therefore you have to do your little *pūjā*.

That is the day the relationship has become real for you, and that is the day you can say that whatever you have been doing up till now has been transformed into prayer. Prayer is the language that has makes the connection with *Bhagavān* real.

Question: Swaminiji, I want to know how long should one pray.

Answer: There are no rules about this these days. In the Vedic times, one had to do all the religious karmas that were prescribed, and therefore, the entire day was spent in prayer. Nowadays life runs according to one's convenience. In America, for instance, all religious ceremonies, festivals, and *pūjās*, regardless of when they occur, are only celebrated during weekends, as no one has time during the weekdays. Perhaps funerary rites are the only exception, as Lord Yama does not follow the weekend rule for harvesting *jīvas*.

Given this situation, one can have a minimum daily *pūjā* that one can afford to do. On some days you need more time, especially in difficult or desperate situations, as it takes longer to reach that place of authentic communion with *Bhagavān*. We do not have a specific length for prayer. We have the *Śrī*

Rudram, which is a long prayer, and we have the shortest *śāntimantra,* a five-word prayer.

> ॐ भद्रं नो अपिवातय मनः ॥
>
> *Oh bhadram no apivātaya manaḥ* ॥
>
> (O Agni!) orient our minds towards the most auspicious end (*mokṣa*). ॥ ṚV 10.20.1 ॥

Question: I had a question about disease and the types of prayer to cure diseases. How can we use prayer efficaciously to be free of disease?

Answer: In the Vedas, especially in the *Atharvaveda,* there are tailor-made prayers for various kinds of diseases. There is a class of hymns known as *Bhaiṣajya-Sukta,* which prescribe elaborate mantras, charms, and rituals for curing airborne diseases like the flu, water-borne diseases like cholera, pest-borne diseases like the plague, various forms of mental illnesses, and illness due to being possessed by spirits, etc. All the Vedas have mantras for health and well-being. In the *śāntimantra* of the Vedas also, we pray for having optimal mental and physical health to enable us to pursue knowledge.

If you do not have access to these rituals, you can rely on the *mahāmṛtyuñjaya* mantra:

> ॐ त्र्यम्बकं यजामहे सुगन्धिम्पुष्टिवर्धनम् ।
> उर्वारुकमिव बन्धनान्मृत्योर्मुक्षीय माऽमृतात् ॥
>
> ***ॐ tryambakaṃ yajāmahe sugandhim puṣṭi-vardhanam । urvārukamiva bandhanān mṛtyor mukṣīya ma'mṛtat.*** ॥
>
> We worship the fragrant three-eyed one, the augmenter of prosperity. Release us from death with the ease of the gourd separating from the vine, but not from immortality. ॥ ṚV 7.59.12 ॥

For this ritual, you can fill a *kalaśa*-pot with water, close the mouth of the pot with a coconut and some leaves, and then chant the mantra with devotion 108 times. The water absorbs the essence and intention of the *mantras*, acting as a potent mantra-conductor. You can then sprinkle the mantra-incanted water on the patient, and also have the person bathe in it.

We have a very sophisticated understanding of *Īśvara* in the tradition. We look upon *Īśvara* from three standpoints: *adhideva,* centered on the *devas, adhibhūta,* centered on the elements, from which everything comes, and *adhyātma* centered on the body-mind-complex. For example, the eyes are a manifestation of *Īśvara* as *adhyātma*. The eyes see because of the presence of light, and what is the light? The light of the *devatā* known as *āditya*, the sun. Therefore, the sun becomes the presiding deity of sight. This is *Īśvara as āditya* is *adhibhūta*. The law that connects sight in a particular individual, *adhyātma,* with *adhibhūta* is *Īśvara* as *adhideva*. This order is vast enough to include disorder. Therefore, if there are any eye problems, we are asked to chant the *Ādityahṛdaya*, a composition, which is an adoration of the Lord as the sun and contains a beautiful teaching on courage. In the same manner, if there are any hearing problems, we invoke the *digdevatā*, the presiding deities of the directions.

We have a very elaborate and sophisticated way of praying for freedom from diseases. Following this blueprint, when new situations arise, new practices and shrines can be established. For instance, during the AIDS epidemic in the 80s, a Goddess shrine named AIDS-Amma emerged in certain parts of rural South India. People would invoke this Goddess to pray for a cure.

Similarly, for poxes like chickenpox and smallpox, there is Māriamma, the Mother Goddess of all poxes. Worshipping such deities is interesting. You do not want them to "bless" you in the form of the pox; you just want them to not be inimical towards you. It is all very beautiful. For those wishing to study or settle abroad, there is the famous Visa-Ganapati temple in Hyderabad. People throng to this temple, which some say, has a high success rate in securing visas for prospective students and IT personnel desirous of going abroad.

Question: I have heard Pujya Swamiji speak about the beauty of prayer, saying that when the will willingly submits, there is a miracle. When I think about praying, I often desire something different from what is. What exactly am I submitting to when I surrender in prayer?

Answer: The surrender is to whatever one confronts at any given time which cannot be altered. What is, is *Bhagavān*. What cannot be altered in life is placed on the altar of surrender, which is *Bhagavān*. The altar of surrender is known as such, because it has the power to alter the devotee into being more mature, accepting and accommodative.

Sometimes, surrender can come out of a sense of desperation when all other options are closed off. When prayer becomes a serious issue, there is already a submission. It involves submitting to the helplessness of a particular *rāga* or *dveṣa,* strong preferences and prejudices, over which one has no control. *Rāga-dveṣa* wreak havoc on the mind because they create a terrible pressure for instant gratification. That is why the Bhagavad-Gita says:

> **शक्नोतीहैव यः सोढुं प्राक्शरीरविमोक्षणात् ।**
> **कामक्रोधोद्भवं वेगं स युक्तः स सुखी नरः ॥**
>
> *śaknotīhaiva yaḥ soḍhuṃ prākśarīravimokṣaṇāt* I
> *kāmakrodhodbhavaṃ vegaṃ sa yuktaḥ sa sukhī naraḥ* II
>
> The one who is capable of not succumbing to the pressure created by desire and anger in this life itself before leaving the body is a person who is emotionally mature and happy.
>
> II BG 5.23 II

When you have exhausted all options and nothing works, the altar of surrender becomes the last frontier of solace and hope. You are submitting to something bigger than that particular *rāga* or *dveṣa*, that has you in its grip. You are submitting to the psychological order of the Lord.

First, there is the understanding that *rāga-dveṣa* exist in every *antaḥkaraṇa*, and therefore, you are not an exception. Once you see this, it is no longer your *rāga-dveṣa;* you no longer own it. You have broadened the horizon of your understanding to see *Bhagavān* as manifest in the form of the vast psychological order, which pervades everyone's emotions, including your own. In so doing, you have sanctified the *rāga-dveṣa,* you have *"Īśvarized"* it. With this step, you are capable of being more objective to the situation at hand, and kinder with yourself. You can pray for the difficult emotions to heal, and for inappropriate desires to dissipate. The *dṛṣṭaphala* is immediate relief. A desire that is not acted upon causes frustration. Prayer is an action; acting on your wish means you have done something and then let it go. It is not in your hands anymore, thank God, and that is where the relief comes from. The submission brings that relief.

Pujya Swamiji said that only in prayer– and in reaching-out actions, such as charity– is the will totally free. In all other actions, the will is bound up in the *rāga-dveṣas*. No matter how desperate one is, one does not have to pray. One can rob a bank, or engage in other forms of *adharma*. Yet one chooses to pray, and therefore, in prayer, the will willingly submits.

Question: How do I know how much *puṇya* is there in my *karmic* bank account? As I study Vedanta, more and more, I am worried that I am not doing much to generate more *puṇya*.

Answer: Ah, this is an interesting problem, is it not? Nobody knows what is in the karmic bank account. Only Citragupta knows. Citragupta is *Bhagavān* in the form of the accountant, who keeps the *pāpa* and *puṇya* records of all the *jīvas*. As one studies Vedanta it is natural to want to move away from all this. Now, one has to cultivate a strong resolve and say "I am not going to concern myself so much about getting *puṇya*. I am just going to follow Vedanta because the mind is naturally moving away from long *pūjās* and *homās*."

Here is a big secret. Once you come under the umbrella of Vedanta, you do not have to do anything special to generate *puṇya*. Each time you listen to a Vedanta class, you get *puṇya*. If you want more *puṇya,* then listen to more classes. If you share your knowledge with others also, you get *puṇya*. Spending time in this manner, not only do you get *puṇya*, you also get contentment. As the Bhagavad-Gita says:

> **मच्चित्ता मद्गतप्राणा बोधयन्तः परस्परम्।**
> **कथयन्तश्च मां नित्यं तुष्यन्ति च रमन्ति च॥**
> ***maccittā madgataprāṇāḥ bodhayantaḥ parasparam Ikathayantaśca māṁ nityaṃ tuṣyanti ca ramanti ca* II**
>
> With their hearts fixed on me, and their lives given to me, they (my devotees) remain contented reveling in me and teaching about me, and conversing about my glories.
>
> II BG 10.9 II

It is good to spend one's time always talking about Vedanta, contemplating upon the words of the Upanishads, and mutually discussing Vedanta with others. As a result, you might find you have fewer friends, but that might just be *Bhagavatprasāda*, protecting you from all that you are wanting to leave behind.

Chapter 7
Internal and External Practices

Meditation and the Wandering Mind

Question: My mind wanders too much even in guided meditation. How can I focus during meditation? When I sit, I cannot concentrate for more than a few minutes.

Answer: We cannot blame the mind for wandering. Its nature is to keep moving. If the mind were to be stationary, neither perception nor action would be possible. Therefore the mind has to be moving constantly.

You can start with the practice of One-Minute-Meditation. Just meditate for one minute. You can endure almost anything for a minute, even the worst discomfort, knowing it is only for a short time. So, imagine how much easier it is to meditate for a minute.

Start by watching the mind. This practice is highly effective. If watching the mind feels too challenging, begin by observing your breath. Focusing on the breath calms both the mind and the breathing. After about half a minute, shift your focus to watching the mind. When the minute is up and your timer goes off, you might think, "I was enjoying this. I should do more." Resist that urge. Instead, keep your mind wanting more, like a limited-edition toy that is only available for a short time. This keeps the practice fresh and engaging.

Once you have mastered the one-minute-meditation, do not jump to longer sessions like meditating for 48 minutes straight. Instead, practice one-minute-mediation several times a day, and gradually increase the length. You can even do this at work during breaks. This approach provides intermittent rewards that maintains one's interest and commitment.

Reducing Mental Clutter

Question: Please comment on how mental clutter can be reduced, which prevents the *nitya-anubhava* of *ātman*? How do you attach the mind to *ātman*?

Answer: The mind does not need to be attached to the *ātman,* because the mind is already non-separate from the *ātman*. This would be like forcing oneself to think of God all the time. What would happen? The first thought is of God. The second thought also is of God. The third thought is also of God. And then what? You might start with "God," but then you see a dog and naturally the mind thinks of the dog. Suddenly, God becomes a dog! This does not work, as *ātman, Īśvara,* is not an object of thought. The *ātman* being yourself cannot be enclosed in a thought. God is you, *Bhagavān* is you, *ātman* is you. It is not an object.

The word "attached" presumes that something is "detached." Operating under this assumption, one feels alienated. This feeling is not the reality. A pencil looks bent when placed in a glass of water. However, when you take it out, it is perfectly straight. Similarly, the perceived detachment is *mithyā*, merely an apparent reality. There is no real attachment or detachment. We assume that the *ātman* is something separate that we must unite with. This is not the case. The *ātman* is already you; it is a self-evident, self-established reality. It is yourself. It does not depend on anything else. It is not *sādhya-vastu*, something to be achieved or gained; it is *svataḥ-siddha-vastu*, already evident.

Therefore, the idea that the mind needs to be exclusively attached to *ātman* is unnecessary. Whatever the mind is attached to, is already non-separate from the *ātman*. Wherever you look, you see *ātman*. The *Dṛgdṛśyaviveka* puts it beautifully:

> **यत्र यत्र मनो याति, तत्र तत्र समाधयः।**
>
> ***Yatra yatra mano yāti, tatra tatra samādhayaḥ*** ।
>
> Wherever the mind goes, there is oneness (absence of subject-object duality).
>
> ॥ DDV 30 ॥

This means that there is no such thing as *anātman*; there is only *ātman*. Everything you see is *ātman* in a particular name and form.

Now, we can look at the first part of the question: How do you reduce mental clutter?

Mental clutter includes *rāga-dveṣa*– strong desires, prejudices, and preferences. There is nothing inherently wrong with desire, but when the desire is in the driving seat and calls all the shots, it is a problem. Desires are a manifestation of the Lord within the *antaḥkaraṇa,* therefore, as long as they do not transgress dharma, you can have as many desires as you want. However, when desires run wild like untamed animals, take over the buddhi, and push you out, then it becomes a problem. Mental clutter can be reduced in two ways: *Antaraṅga-sādhana,* and *Bahiraṅga-sādhana.*

Antaraṅga-sādhana is an inward means of preparing the mind. It includes practices such as meditation, *prāṇāyāma*, contemplation, or sitting quietly with oneself. By quelling the restlessness of the mind, it helps to bring about *citta-naiścalyam,* stability and focus.

The other means is known as *bahiraṅga-sādhana,* outward means. Examples of this are *karmayoga, sevā,* charity, or pilgrimage.

When we engage in serving others, the heart expands. One is no longer obsessed with one's own complaints. This fosters objectivity and leads to *citta-śuddhi,* purity of mind. The purification of the mind and senses prepares one to receive and abide in the sacred teachings of the "I" as whole and free.

Question: You had mentioned in one of the retreats that the mind needs to be a servant in the aid of this knowledge, and, not the king. Please help me understand how to do this. I know meditation helps, but I need more tools in my toolbox to figure that out.

Answer: Training the mind is just like training a puppy not to get on the furniture. Every new dog owner at first thinks that the puppy should not be on the sofa or the bed. After a few days, we find that the owner is sitting on the floor while the puppy is enjoying itself sitting in the owner's favorite chair.

In the USA, there are obedience schools for dogs. Once, during my travels, I met people who run a dog obedience school. I asked them what happens there, and how they teach the dogs to be obedient. This couple said that the obedience school is not really for the dogs; on the contrary, it is for the human beings. They said that the dogs do not need schools, because they are very consistent. It is the human being who is inconsistent. The pet owner at one point in time says to the dog, "Come, come, you are 'cho chweet', you are so cute! Just this once you can sit with me on the couch." Another time the same person goes berserk and yells at the dog, rolled-up newspaper in hand: "No no no! Get off the sofa! Bad boy!" The poor dog is utterly confused.

Theey said, "Therefore, we train the pet owners to be consistent in their commands. We actually train human beings, but I suppose it is known as a dog school so that the human beings do not feel offended."

Just as one has to be consistent in training the dog, so too the same consistency has to be applied in training the dogged mind. You have to be the master, and practice having a say over the ways of the mind. Lord Krishna's advice in the Bhagavad-Gita is very pertinent in this context:

असंशयं महाबाहो मनो दुर्निग्रहं चलम्।
अभ्यासेन तु कौन्तेय वैराग्येण च गृह्यते ॥

asaṃśayaṃ mahābāho mano durnigrahaṃ calam
***abhyāsena tu kaunteya vairāgyeṇa ca gṛihyate* II**

Doubtlessly, O Mighty Armed One, the mind is difficult to restrain; however, with repeated practice and dispassion, it can be trained.

II BG 6.35 II

It is important to purify and train the *antaḥkaraṇa* because it is the place where Brahman as the truth of oneself is recognized. However the mind is not the author of *brahmavidyā;* it is not the agent of this knowledge. Self-knowledge takes place in the mind, but not by the mind. For this reason, the mind has to be ready and receptive. The mind should be in service of this knowledge.

The mind is in cahoots with the *ahaṅkāra*, the I-notion. The *ahaṅkāra* is a trickster. Identifying with mind, it convinces it to masquerade as the agent of *brahmajñāna*. Therefore, one has to be consistent about repeatedly dethroning the mind from trying to control the process by which the assimilation of knowledge takes place. The practice of *japa* helps to stabilize the mind and reduce distractions, while, *karmayoga* helps with the cultivation of dispassion by managing one's *rāga-dveṣa.*

Question: I have two questions. Does Vedanta talk about astrology? Do you have any practical suggestions or tips for improving one's meditation practice to reach subtler realms?

Answer: Astrology, *jyotiṣa,* is an *aṅga* of the Veda. It is known as a *Vedāṅga*. It is part of the Veda, so it has Vedic validity.

Jyotiṣa is a highly regarded branch of knowledge, but some people use it as an oracle to predict their future. An astrology reading should not be a prison sentence. The horoscope is, at best, an exciting study of the possibilities that one can encounter in one's lifetime. Let not the 'horror-scope' be the bars of a cage that imprisons you.

For a beginner, meditation is best practiced in small increments. If you tell yourself, "I am going to sit for 48 minutes." then you will not even be able to sit for 4 minutes, because this is how the mind is. It says, "you are going to sit for 48 minutes? I am going to make sure you don't." Therefore, it is best to start small. Start by chanting the *japa*. *Japa* is very important. Start by chanting the *mantra* for just half a minute, or for one minute. We have already spoken about the one-minute-meditation technique. It is effective for people who are easily distracted.

The point in meditation is quality, not quantity. Quantity will come on its own. Our job is to focus on centering the mind. When distractions happen– and they certainly will– the point is not to feel self-judgmental for going away from the *mantra*. We gently bring the mind back, like a mother bringing a toddler, who is straying onto the main road, back to safety.

Then, we look at when distractions happen. Distractions cannot happen while chanting the *mantra*. While saying "*Oṁ namaḥ śivāya*," the mind is occupied. So, when does the distraction happen? In between two "*Oṁ namaḥ śivāya*" chants, there is a space where one can think of things other than the mantra. Here, we practice closely observing the silence in the spaces between the chants. When you do this, it becomes meditation. To use your words, the meditation becomes more subtle and more sublime.

Question: My question is about how to control the mind. It is very difficult to control the mind. How do I achieve one-point focus instead of having several interests? I feel attracted to the truth in all religions. I study Buddhism as well, and Vedanta really speaks to my heart. Then I think that perhaps I should be with Christianity as Vedanta is difficult.

Answer: The first thing we need to understand is that we do not control the mind. You do not control anything. You can manage the mind.

The next thing to know is that Vedanta is not in competition with Buddhism or Christianity. Vedanta is you. It is not a religion; it is not even a way of life. It is a body of knowledge that is meant for everyone, regardless of whether they are Buddhists, Jewish, Catholic, or from any other tradition. Everyone who is afflicted by sorrow and fear needs this teaching, because there is no such thing as "Christian sorrow," which is different from "Buddhist sorrow." You have recognized this fact, and that is why Vedanta speaks to your heart. Vedanta is not going to make you less of a Christian.

Sevā and Karmayoga

Question: In my profession, I was a pediatrician, and now that I have stopped working and started taking these classes, I am always wanting to know how we can reach children. How can we teach Vedanta philosophy to children in a world dominated by computers, video games and social media? Kids just do not have the time to learn about spirituality, and I feel like if they were given the opportunity to find more balance in life at a young age, they might not suffer as much. They could deal with their situations with a bigger heart and with less negativity. Are there any resources I can pass on to my nieces and nephews? Are there any books? I am even thinking about possibly writing a book for kids. Though I am not a scholar, I feel like, given my profession of

working with children, this is something I would love to pass on.

Answer: The short answer is that Vedanta is not for children; it is meant for adults. Play is for children, and stories are for children. When adults study Vedanta and behave calmly, their tranquility benefits the children. This does not mean you cannot teach children. There are many stories in the *Purāṇas* and the *Pañcatantra* that children can understand. You can write a book based on these *Purāṇic* stories and *ślokas*. There are many things you can teach them, like chanting. They are very good at chanting and will quickly pick it up. You can tell them a bit of the meaning as well.

Children love to work with their hands. You can have a clay *Gaṇeśa* making workshop. It is very nice. You take a lump of clay, make an egg shape, and then create the ears by pressing the sides. Turn it over, shape the trunk, and use a matchstick to make lines on the trunk and add some seeds for the eyes. Then you have your *Gaṇeśa*. These are the kind of things you can teach children.

As for the spirit of the question, which is asks: Can we ward off all the pain and suffering that children have to undergo in adulthood now itself? The idea that if kids learn Vedanta at age five, they will grow up without pain or sorrow is unrealistic. A verse from the *Bhaja-Govindam*, a Vedanta text attributed to Adi Shankara, discusses the problem of the right age for the study of Vedanta. No age is the right age, and no age is the wrong age either:

> **बालस्तावत्क्रीडासक्तः तरुणस्तावत्तरुणीरक्तः।**
> **वृद्धस्तावच्चिन्तामग्नः परमे ब्रह्मणि कोऽपि न लग्नः॥**
>
> *bālastāvatkrīḍāsaktaḥ taruṇastāvattaruṇīraktaḥ* ।
> *vṛddhastāvaccintāmagnaḥ pare brahmaṇi ko'pi na lagnaḥ* ॥
>
> The child is addicted to play; the young person is only interested in another young person, the elderly person is full of worries and woes and, therefore, no one is ready to be committed to understanding Brahman.
>
> ॥ Bh.G 7 ॥

Which is the correct age to study Vedanta? Five? But, alas, children are not interested in Vedanta. They are only interested in playing with their toys. Then, perhaps one should study Vedanta as a young adult. This sounds like a good idea, but the young person is interested only in pursuing another young adult, not Vedanta. Alright, okay, perhaps we should finish our jobs, fulfill a few desires, retire, and then go to a teacher at age 72. Maybe that is the right time for Vedanta. Elderly people are usually worried about what is going to happen to their property after they die. Who will get it? Will their children get along? They already do not get along. What will happen after they go? How will their hard-earned money be handled? Will it be squandered? What will happen to their children? These are the obsessions of the elderly.

In other words, for the study of Vedanta, no age is a good age, and every age is a good age. If the preparedness is there, then one could be like Nachiketa, who was a young boy already ready for Vedanta, or one could be like the elderly sages sitting at the feet of Lord *Dakṣiṇāmūrti*.

Once readiness is there, the knowledge comes. Therefore it is not about the age; it is about having mental tranquility, well-managed *rāga-dveṣa*, and a relatively cheerful disposition. It depends, not on the age, but on the readiness of the heart and mind. How is the readiness gained? It is gained through *karmayoga* and meditation. Meditation provides focus and determination to follow this path, while *karmayoga* neutralizes strong preferences lurking in the heart.

There is a wonderful set of books from our ashram called *Pūrṇa-Vidyā*, which teaches children a bit of what they can understand. It includes a summary of the Bhagavad-Gita for teenagers and other aspects like *Purāṇas*. It even has lesson plans, so wherever you are, you can start a children's group. You can get it from the ashram in Saylorsburg, PA.

Question: Since I was young, I have seen the weaknesses and incapabilities of people. I never considered what I did to people and what kind of karma this brings to me. Did I do the right thing Swaminiji? I am a social worker. I take care of and find solutions, but I do not want to overstep. They have to find it themselves.

Answer: This is a very good realization and understanding. Two things I would suggest. First, if it bothers you, you can have a small atonement and say, "*Īśvara*, take care of all of them, and let whatever I said or did not come back to me."

Second, going forward, you can approach things differently. When people come for advice, it is not that they do not know; they just feel uncertain. Most people want to be listened to. When we learn the art of listening deeply, people seek their own solutions.

Cultivating Healthy Boundaries

Question: I was wondering if you could talk about how to serve and love without becoming depleted in a relationship and at work. If one does burn out, what would you recommend?

Answer: We need to have healthy limits. This is very important in any kind of caregiving work or outreach, including with one's own family members. Healthy boundaries cannot come from outside; they must come from within. You have to be in touch with yourself, with knowing how much you can give and what is realistic for you each day. You should be able to say, "Not now, maybe another time." Healthy boundaries come from spending time with oneself. When you have inner space, when you make the room, they organically reveal themselves. That is the first thing.

The second thing is to learn to give ungrudgingly by understanding service as an act of worship. It is important not to overdo, as exhaustion can lead to a feeling of resentment. When one does not respect one's own boundaries, one can become cranky. Seeing service as an act of worship really changes the perspective so that one can willingly engage in *sevā*.

If one cannot do something as an act of worship, it is better to wait until one is in the right mindset to give, to serve. Cultivating this authenticity is also part of having healthy boundaries. Finally, it is important to be honest with oneself and look within for the presence of unmanageable expectations as a result of one's service.

If I am serving people lovingly, I expect them to be appreciative. That is a normal expectation. I expect them to be appreciative, receptive, and reciprocative. These are all okay to have, but I have to also understand that often these expectations will not be met. I have to be willing not to take that as a personal slight. Each time I am in a service-oriented calling or profession, I must understand this very well: when my efforts are not appreciated, I should not take it personally. How else should I take it? I must take it as an opportunity for my own growth. I must be ready to drop expectations more and more by seeing whatever comes as a result of the service as *prasāda*. When *prasāda* is given what do you do? You receive it, touch it to your heart and eyes, and eat it. You do not say, "Why no laddoos today? That one got two banana pieces; I got only one. Why this partiality? I am a frequent donor to this temple. I demand *banana-prasāda*." We do not say that. We take whatever is given, and eat it. This is a metaphor for life.

Whatever comes, I receive it reverentially, with glad acceptance. That is how I grow. Otherwise, there is no emotional growth.

Chapter 8
CULTIVATING DISCIPLESHIP

Devotion

Question: What does devotion mean? Does it have to be directed to a specific entity, or is it your belief in compassion? Can it be kindness? Love? What are we devoted to?

Answer: You are devoted to the practice of seeing everything you do as an act of worship to God. That is what you are devoted to. Whatever you do– eating, drinking, sleeping, serving– everything is an act of worship. The recipient of all your actions is *Bhagavān*, *Īśvara*, however you may think of or invoke God. That is what devotion is. Of course, compassion is part of it. Kindness is part of it. Love is part of it. It is all included.

Question: How can one increase devotion? Even though we have talked about it extensively and have the knowledge, it still

feels like there is much more to do to truly open the heart.

Answer: Take every opportunity to practice devotion. Devotion should not be limited to *pūjā* or worship time. One should transition from being a person who prays to being a prayerful person. For a person who prays, prayer is a discrete act. For a prayerful person, the attitude with which every act is performed is imbued with devotion.

Everything should be done carefully and devotionally as though it is *pūjā*. This is the essence of *karmayoga*. Whether it is cooking, cleaning, or any mundane task, we do it all in this spirit of service. There will be days when resentment or anger comes. When that happens, we can take a deep breath, and just smile. Even if you do not want to smile, smile, and slowly the teeth will unclench. Smile and breathe, even if you do not feel like it.

Dispassion

Question: My question is about the law of attraction, and balancing non-attachment to things while also wanting a husband. Should I create a vision board with magazine images of the perfect man I want? Is that okay? It sounds interesting, and I want to see how it goes. However, it seems contradictory to the will of God, which emphasizes non-attachment. I do not understand this.

Answer: This law of attraction business is best understood as a prayer. Then it makes sense. It is not that you are manifesting anything– the desire is already there, and you are putting it together. You are cutting the face from one magazine, the body from another, and the legs from yet another. Internally, he should be of a *sattvic* disposition, and must be interested in pursuing Vedanta!

You do not see it as you manifesting, you see it as the agent who is manifesting because you are not clear, and you do not know. You see it as a manifestation, and *Bhagavān* manifests in you and is helping. Say to

Bhagavān, "Can you please include a few things here, please make him into a decent person?" Now it is just saying, "I really want this whole lot; please help me here." There is nothing wrong with being clear and candid. After you put this ideal man on the altar, you say "*svāḥā*."

Svāḥā is an expression of letting go. We tell *Īśvara*, "Now it is in your hands. I am going to stop thinking about it. I let go." You say that. Inside, you may still be holding on, but at least you said "*svāḥā*." You have come one step closer to letting go.

This is what we do in the fire ritual. When we have a *homā*, we say, "*Svāḥā, indrāya svāḥā. idaṃ na mama*" (this is not for me, but for Lord Indra). This is an exercise in letting that desire go free. Good luck in your quest in finding a suitable life partner.

Question: When you are super passionate and alive, there is this component of dispassion. Can you talk about it?

Answer: We do not aim to be super-passionate. Dispassion does not mean disengagement or apathy. It is not sitting back and doing nothing. Dispassion does not mean that we do not act. Rather, it means that one engages in actions without being invested in a particular outcome. Although I may have a preference, when faced with an outcome that I did not want, I learn to adjust my expectations in keeping with the outcome. Expectations are subjective, while the outcome is objective. I have to learn to live with what is objective. That is called growth. It is overcoming strong preferences and prejudices known as *rāga* and *dveṣa*.

Dispassion means growing into a place of accepting whatever comes as *prasāda* from *Bhagavān*. It is called *prasāda-buddhi*. I will not say it is non-attachment because we are never truly attached to begin with. The *ātman* is ever *asaṅga*, naturally uninvolved with everything. The correct term here is *vairāgya*, the absence of strong preferences for a particular outcome. It involves adjusting preferences and prejudices to align with the outcome.

This adjustment makes one grow. One adapts the preferences in light of whatever has come. Whatever has come is *Bhagavān's* will. This is called *prasāda-buddhi*, the intellect accepting everything as *prasāda*, glad acceptance.

Self-Discipline

Question: I do not understand why even though we know what we need to do to grow, we do not do it. Speaking from my own experience, I know what I need to do to grow emotionally, which would allow me to give more time to Vedanta. I do not understand why we do not do what we know is good for us.

Answer: Arjuna has a similar question in the Bhagavad-Gita:

> अथ केन प्रयुक्तोऽयं पापं चरति पूरुषः।
> अनिच्छन्नपि वार्ष्णेय बलादिव नियोजितः॥
>
> *atha kena prayukto'yaṁ pāpaṃ carati pūruṣaḥ* I
> *anicchannapi vārṣṇeya balādiva niyojitaḥ* II
>
> Impelled by which force does the person, even without wishing to do so, engage in wrong-doing

as though led there by force? II BG 3.36 II

What force compels a person to indulge in wrongdoing, despite knowing it is against their
best interests? Why do we sabotage ourselves by engaging in actions that contradict our own wisdom and well-being?

It feels as though we are driven by an external force, compelling us to do things we know are not good for us. Why do we not listen to our best instincts and the highest wisdom within ourselves? Why do we continue to make choices that we know are detrimental to our growth?

Lord Krishna's answer to this dilemma is very insightful:

> काम एष क्रोध एष रजोगुणसमुद्भवः।
> महाशनो महापाप्मा विद्ध्येनमिह वैरिणम्॥
>
> *kāma eṣa krodha eṣa rajoguṇasamudbhavaḥ* I
> *mahāśano mahāpāpmā viddhyenamiha vairiṇam* II
>
> This desire and this anger, born of a *rajasic* disposition, are omnivores and the worst offenders. Know them to be inimical (to your growth). II BG 3.37 II

Lord Krishna says the desires are unstoppable. Well-entrenched, binding desires exert a pressure known in Sanskrit as *vega*. This pressure demands fulfillment. When a desire is thwarted, it becomes the cause of sorrow and frustration. Anger often arises because something has not gone as one wished. An unfulfilled *kāma* turns into *krodha*. This is easy to understand.

This dynamic is born of *rajas*, the principle of motion and activity, which, when unbalanced, leads to anger, intolerance, even violence. These are the characteristics of *rajo-guṇa*. Lord Krishna describes desire as *mahāpāpman*– the worst offender. He also calls it *mahāśana*, an omnivore that consumes everything, starting with your sanity. Desire turns into anger and consumes everything, including your peace of mind. It devours relentlessly, as it has a voracious appetite and never stops wanting more. *Kāma* can never be satisfied because it has no end.

This brings us back to our favorite topic: *rāga* and *dveṣa*. The key to managing them is through practicing delayed gratification. If you tell yourself, "I am never going to have it," you might end up wanting it even more. So, instead, say, "I will have just one." If you want three, have one. If you want one, have just a third. And if you want it right now, wait for three hours. By telling yourself, "This is mine, I am not going to give it to anyone, but I will have it later," you create a space for the impulses to feel safe. Keep yourself busy in the meantime. Often, after three hours, you may forget about the object of desire entirely. The next day, you might think, "Oh, I forgot to eat that." And after three days, the craving may lessen significantly. We need to be gentle with ourselves. With patience and gradual steps, we can overcome our impulses.

Question: How can I be consistent and accountable? I get distracted and do not follow up on my plans. How do I develop a greater resolve to go to the gym etc.?

Answer: An effective strategy is to reward yourself afterwards. For instance, you could say, "I will go to the gym, and after that, I will treat myself to something I love" such as stopping by a place you enjoy, spending time on a hobby, calling a friend you have not spoken to in a while, or visiting a spot you like. Promise yourself these small rewards after completing your gym session or task. This approach makes the activity more appealing and helps you stay consistent.

Question: There are times when you are pretty motivated to do things the right way, but what to do when you know what you are doing is not right, and yet you still cannot stop?

Answer: There are times when one is motivated to go with the flow– one runs when one is motivated. There are other times when one feels like a water buffalo. Once it sits submerged in a swamp-puddle, it just cannot be coaxed out. What to do? Sit, that is all. Sit for some time and then tell yourself a very simple truth: even the water buffalo has to eat and drink. Since I am just feeling like a water buffalo, but without being a water-buffalo, I have to cook for myself and then clean up also. In this way, we motivate ourselves little by little.

Sometimes, the lack of motivation is due to a painful memory being triggered. One may not know what it is, so it might be nice to write it out. Writing regularly in a journal is a very fruitful practice, yielding good insights.

Question: I have been described as a fixer, someone who fixes situations. I have done it for my family and friends. If something is wrong, they call me. I appreciate that and like being capable of it, but it is a burden, and I cannot always be good at it. Do you have advice for that?

Answer: I commend you for even discussing this topic. You must be marvelous at fixing things, and at the same time, I am happy to hear you say that it feels like a burden. It really is because it involves managing a lot of people's lives and expectations.

You can give yourself the permission to drop it and to say to your relatives, friends, and family, "Right now, I do not think I can do this. I do not have the answers, and I do not know the best course of action." You can say that. Start by saying, "I can take a look at it, but I do not think I will solve it. I am not able to solve it."

Acknowledging the presence of *Īśvara* in one's life really helps. It does not take too long to see that the talents and skills one has are all given, and therefore one cannot claim ownership of anything, not even of one's own body.

I know a grandmother who lives in Washington D.C. She had two grandchildren and right from the start, she instilled in them that everything was given by Lord Krishna and everything was being done by Lord Krishna. She taught them that they were not doing anything; Krishna was doing it, and Krishna was the agent of everyone's action.

Once there was a big celebration at a temple in Washington, D.C., and she had to make some fried bread called puris. She had to make 300 of them. She managed to make them, and everything went well. The next day, a friend called her, and the lady said, "Oh! everything is hurting. My arms are hurting, head is hurting. You do not know this because you are out of town, but I made 300 puris. I kneaded the dough, flattened all of them out, and fried each one of them. A total of 300 puris. OMG, I am so tired and in so much pain."

The three-year-old grandson, who was overhearing this conversation said, "Grandma! If Krishna is the one who is making the puris, why are you in pain?"

She realized that there is no room to not walk the
talk. She had to walk the talk. That is why I say if children or grandchildren are around, they quicken the path to *mokṣa*.

Spiritual Growth

Question: **Swaminiji, when everything you teach is working on me, causing a shift in my thinking and perception, why do I still long for all the things I used to do and enjoy?**

Answer: There are many versions of this question. People often say, "After listening to the teachings, I feel transformed. The old things I used to enjoy, like friends, movies, gossiping, parties and dinners, do not interest me much. But then, I am not that much interested in Vedanta either. I am betwixt and between. What should I do?" The Bhagavad-Gita says:

> **विषया विनिवर्तन्ते निराहारस्य देहिनः।**
> **रसवर्जं रसोऽप्यस्य परं दृष्ट्वा निवर्तते॥**
>
> ***viṣayā vinivartante nirāhārasya dehinaḥ*** **I**
> ***rasavarjaṃ raso'pyasya paraṃ dṛṣṭvā nivartate*** **II**
>
> For the one who does not feed the senses, they return to oneself, leaving behind a longing for the objects. When Brahman is known as oneself, the longing also goes away. II BG 2.59 II

We follow the baby and candy logic. If you want to talk of how easy a task is, you use the expression, "It is like taking candy from a baby." To this I would say that whoever came up with this saying must not have had a baby. If you want to take candy from the hands of a baby, it is not that easy. The baby has a strong grip and even stronger vocal cords. So, how do you get candy out of a baby's hand? You give the baby something else. Hold a teddy bear near the baby; it will grab the teddy bear, and the candy will fall to the ground on its own accord. How do you take away the teddy bear? You have to give it another toy. That is how life is. Throughout one replaces one object with another. When a new, shiny object is offered, the older object loses its appeal.

This is what the Bhagavad-Gita says. Initially, you drop things that no longer serve you. It is not even that you actively drop them; they drop away by themselves. You find yourself not calling people who are– to use a trendy word– "toxic." You do not want to hang out with people with whom you have dysfunctional relationships. You no longer prioritize those relationships. However, there is still a lingering desire in your heart.

You want to bring out the best in yourself, so why would you hang out with people who constantly complain, especially when you want to stop complaining and help others? This change happens naturally, without any force. These outings, meetings, and gatherings no longer amuse you. Yet, there remains a residual desire for them. You might see a group of people and think, "Oh, I wish I were a part of that. I wish I could go there."

One person came to me and said that thanks to Vedanta, nobody was inviting her for parties. Then, one day this lady received an invitation. She was very happy and wrote to me, saying, "Finally, I got an invitation for a Thanksgiving gathering. I am going to spend the whole afternoon and evening with this family." The next time I saw her, I asked how it was. She said, "Oh, I was bored out of my wits. It was just terrible. They did not know what to talk about with me, and I could not handle it. It was impolite to leave, especially since I had practically begged to be invited."

The lurking desire is for the idea of the thing, not the thing itself. Although I have distanced myself from it and am no longer feeding that desire, its residue is still there. However, the desire dissipates when the determination and focus are squarely on knowing Brahman.

When you fully pursue this knowledge, the lingering residual desire for something or the other disappears. You might then think, "Why can't I be 'unenlightened' now so that I can enjoy the things I used to in the past?"

It is too late for that. You can unfriend someone on Facebook, but you cannot become self-ignorant again. You are on a path of total transformation, and so you keep at it. Sometimes you might feel like second-guessing yourself, thinking maybe you are not doing it right. This is why we rely on satsang, the company of like-minded people, even on Zoom.

In fact, it is said that you only get one-fourth of this knowledge from the teacher. What about the other three-fourths? You get a quarter from fellow students who are asking questions. It might not be your question, but it speaks to you even though somebody else asks it. That is the point. Another fourth you get while standing under the shower. Why? Because the head is having some blood supply; hot water is giving a nice massage to the brain cells. You also get some "aha" moments by yourself in meditation, while ruminating on these teachings. The last quarter comes on its own time.

You cannot force a rosebud to open by saying "Come on, Buddy, bloom, the Swami is coming to my house, and I want to give you to the Swami!" Likewise, you cannot will yourself to have this knowledge according to your own schedule. In time, things will happen naturally. We learn together, ask questions, and study together. That is the way to ward off alienation.

Question: What is the best way to be on the path of Vedanta study and keep it going?

Answer: Constant and steady exposure to the teachings is the only way to keep it going continuously. There is no other way.

Question: Can you speak a little about how to balance and keep your spiritual path as the primary focus while staying aware of current events, and being part of and helping the world? I find it challenging to remain relevant in the world and still focus on a spiritual path.

Answer: It is not easy because when we take the unreal to be real, the real appears to be come irrelevant. This makes pursuing a spiritual path when one has a strong sense of duty to do good in the world challenging. There is a beautiful story relating to this difficulty about one King Janaka, an enlightened monarch.

One day a *brahmacārin* arrived at the palace for instruction. The king gave him two lamps filled to the brim with oil, and asked him to tour the whole palace and return without spilling a single drop of oil. The *brahmacārin* focused intensely on his task, and returned to the king without spilling any oil. The boy, very pleased with himself, expected the king to shower him with blessings and praise. But before he could speak, however, the king surprised him by asking him to describe the frescoes in a particular room of the palace in detail. The *brahmacārin*, having been totally preoccupied with not spilling the oil, could not answer. The king then told him to repeat the task, emphasizing that the challenge lay in maintaining both focus and awareness.

The more one is established in truth of the self, the more everything becomes enjoyable. Equipped with the vision of Vedanta, nothing is stressful. We find that everything is amusing. We do not take things too seriously, and are able to laugh at ourselves.

Knowing that everything is *mithyā*, we do not take things too seriously, but at the same time, we do not neglect our duties or procrastinate. We cannot be sloppy; care must be taken in the performance of actions. At the same time, we understand that we have a healthy relationship with the world because the world is not separate from God. You see God in the world, and you see God in everything. You *Īśvarize* the *jagat*.

We should check in with our body from time to time. If the shoulders get tense and the fists clench, we have to take the time to remind ourselves that we are naturally free of tension. Sometimes, we may need little reminders. For instance, Buddhists have a bell that rings periodically in the monastery. Its sole purpose for all the people living there is to stop whatever they are doing and take the time to come back to the present moment. The bell is an invitation to return to yourself.

If this helps to stay present, one can replicate that by setting random reminders on the cell phone. When the phone dings, one can take the time to slow down, unclench the fists, smile, and take a few deep breaths. Breathing is free, so we can freely breathe and enjoy just being in the moment. This practice helps to enjoy the present and forget what made one upset. Eventually, with self-knowledge, one will be able to enjoy the palace tour without spilling the oil.

Question: Let us say someone has fallen off the righteous path, and is now in *adharma*, doing wrong things. How can we use Vedanta to get such a person back on the right path? How can we make the person see the error of their ways.

Answer: It is not the purpose of Vedanta to put anyone on the right path. One has to be on the right path first to gain this knowledge. If someone has taken to a life of wrong actions, you can help them and tell them, but if they are not ready to see the error of their ways, they have to go through their own journey. You can pray for *Bhagavān* to bring them back. Perhaps they need this knowledge more than anyone else, but until they return from their wrongdoing, there is no point in teaching them. It is like encouraging a pickpocket to attend a Vedanta class. The pickpocket is very focused. He thinks, "Let us see what all people have brought to the class and where they are stashing their handbags and wallets." Then he thinks "Oh, there is a joke in the class, and everyone is laughing and distracted. This is my time to act." The *Kaṭhopaniṣad* clearly states that those who have not given up *adharma*, and those who are not otherwise ready, can never gain this knowledge:

नाविरतो दुश्चरितात् नाशान्तो नासमाहितः।
नाशान्तमानसो वापि प्रज्ञानेनैनमाप्नुयात्॥

nāvirato duścaritāt nāśānto nāsamāhitaḥ I
nāśānta-mānaso vāpi nti-mantra āpnuyāt II

Neither the one who has not desisted from *adharma*, nor one is restless, whose senses are discomposed, nor one who is not steadfast nor one whose mind is restless can gain this (*ātman*) through self-knowledge.

II KU 1.2.24 II

Question: What kind of daily *sādhana* needs to be done to be on this path?

Answer: *Śravaṇa*, *śravaṇa*, and more *śravaṇa*. Keep listening to the teachings because one time is not enough. We have to keep listening because the habitual patterns are so dense that they take us away from where we need to be. It is easy to forget that *śravaṇa* itself is the main *sādhana* for self-knowledge. People often think of *sādhana* as yoga, meditation, or some kind of *tapas*.

Listening to the teachings is itself a *sādhana*. When you listen, if you are here for two hours in the afternoon, one hour in the morning, and one hour in the evening, that means you have done four hours of meditation without even knowing it. If you listen closely, internal transformation takes place as the ignorance is shed. There is determination, focus, and the letting go of *rāga* and *dveṣa*.

Question: Swaminiji, how can one develop his or her witness consciousness?

Answer: The witness is already there. It is you.
You are talking to me now, and you are also observing that you are talking to me, and you are observing that I am responding to you.

You are already the *sākṣin*, observer; the task at hand is to identify with the observer, to reclaim that observer as yourself.

In meditation, when we say, *"Oṁ namaḥ śivāya,"* we bring the mind back to that awareness. *"Oṁ namaḥ śivāya"* is first thought, *"Oṁ namaḥ śivāya"*is second thought, *"Oṁ namaḥ śivāya"* is third thought. Then the fourth thought might be, "Is anything happening?" Then we observe that the mind has slipped from the *japa*, and we realize we need to bring the mind back to the *japa*.

Commitment to the teaching itself helps you bring the mind back. It is like an auto suggestion. Say, you have an important interview the next morning and before going to bed you set the alarm for 5:00AM. Invariably you find yourself waking up a few minutes before it rings. Getting the mind back to witnessing is like an open-eye meditation. We gradually train the mind to return when distracted. That is the whole idea.

Question: When I was a kid, around eight or nine years old, people would often ask, "Oh, why are you so sad?" I would respond, "I am not sad; I am just thinking." I was always thinking about various things, and I have always been that way– constantly questioning and pondering. This tendency does not naturally align with smiling. For example, there is nothing I love more than laughing, but I do not find many opportunities to do so. I am wondering how I can incorporate smiling and laughing into my life, beyond just "faking it until I make it." How can I integrate this into my study and listening to Vedantic thought, considering my habit of constantly thinking and questioning?

Answer: I would begin by laughing at myself for always thinking about things. When we are able to laugh at ourselves, we can laugh at other things as well. "Fake it till you make it" is a very good approach suggested by Pujya Swamiji. If you practice smiling even with clenched teeth, after a while, you will laugh at yourself, and then the teeth will unclench. People tend to live too much in the head, and consequently get alienated from the present. One can start to reconnect by noticing and appreciating small things, by being more aware of the surroundings: the warmth of the shining sun, the feel of the morning breeze on the face, the soft grass growing under the feet. In this way, one understands that one is naturally free of tension, and ultimately, there is nothing to think about.

Question: What is the meaning of surrendering on the spiritual path? Why do I need a guru to gain this knowledge?

Answer: In life, we find that it is easy to have various kinds of gurus– cooking guru, dance guru, stock market guru, life gurus– but when it comes to the most important guru, the one who teaches you how to be free of *saṃsāra*, people succumb to unconscious fear and start having guru-allergy. As soon as we hear the word "surrender," rashes start to appear because we have not understood the meaning of surrender. Generally, people think that surrender means giving up one's own power and following someone, and doing as they say for the rest of the life. The guru says "Sit," and so I sit down; when the guru says "Stand," then I stand up. This is not the spirit of surrender.

In the *Muṇḍakopaniṣad*, there are two criteria mentioned for selecting a teacher. The first criterion that the teacher must be a *śrotriya*, hailing from a sound lineage. A sound lineage is one that does not distort the message of oneness in the Upanishads. The second criterion is that the teacher must be a *brahmaniṣṭha*, committed to Brahman. Since finding a *brahmaniṣṭha* without oneself being a *brahmaniṣṭha* is impossible, we go with the first criterion. Here, one is safe because the teacher who is teaching you was a student just like you, and therefore is not on an ego-trip, claiming, "I am God, but you are not."

The teacher is a scion of the lineage, representing an embodiment of the teaching. You do not surrender to the individual; you surrender to the *śāstra*, which the teacher embodies and amplifies. The teaching provides a new pair of eyes with which you can see yourself. You do not surrender to the person; you surrender to the *pramāṇa*, the means of knowledge, in the form of words that are the Upanishads, which releases one from *saṃsāra*. The teacher is the audiobook of the Upanishads.

Thus, the teacher comes along with the book for free.It is a package deal, and you surrender to the whole package.

Once, I was in Japan with a group of religious leaders at an interfaith gathering. On the last day, the organizers planned a bus tour of Tokyo for all of us. The bus tour came with a very vivacious and enthusiastic tour guide, which we had not expected. Had the tour guide not been present, we would not know the importance of the buildings and monuments that we encountered. This is exactly what the guru is.

If you want to go on an Upanishad trip by yourself, you will not understand anything. You will just trip. However, when the guru is the tour-guide, *artha-sphuraṇa*, the lighting up of the words of the Upanishad that reveal you to be perfect, blemish-free, and limitless, easily takes place. We surrender to the *śāstra*; we surrender because we know that we need help, and we know that without surrendering to the teaching, *saṃsāra* will continue to hold us in its thrall.

Chapter 9
GURU AND GRACE

The Importance of a Preceptor

Question: I heard that the Upanishads were downloaded by the *ṛṣis*. Swaminiji, can we also download an Upanishad from *Bhagavān*?

Answer: Yes, this is possible. We can also "download" an Upanishad, provided our disposition and mindset are exactly like that of the *ṛṣis*. Until that happens, there are many Upanishads already provided for us to study. We can avail of them.

Question: You said that when we encounter words of the teachings, the first impulse is to dismiss them. Why does this happen? How can we absorb knowledge?

Answer: In the beginning of the study, words of the teaching are often dismissed or rejected, because one is already full of manifold notions about oneself, the world, and God. Together, these notions comprise one's infrastructure, which one inevitably brings to the teaching situation. This is an impediment to learning, as a result of which the words of the *śruti* do not touch the person.

The teachings are fielded by intellect and the mind. Backed by the *ahaṅkāra*, the mind mistakes itself to be the agent of this knowledge. In vain, the mind tries to objectify the self. Not only is it a fact that the self cannot be objectified, the self need not be objectified as it is already self-evident. The mind is preoccupied with categorizing self-knowledge, and wondering which box to put it in. In fact, for this knowledge to work, it is the mind that needs to be boxed by the knowledge, pun intended.

As we have seen before, the mind is not an agent, it is a servant of this knowledge. It is a place where knowledge is recognized, just like any other thing in the *jagat* is recognized. It is crucial for us to recognize that the mind is simultaneously *jagataḥ upalabdhisthāna,* and *jagato'dhiṣṭhānasyāpi upalabdhisthāna*. The mind is a place of cognition of the *jagat*, and also the place of cognition of oneself as Brahman, the truth of the *jagat*. To put it differently, the mind is the place where the object and the subject are both cognized.

In the cognition of the *jagat,* the mind has to objectify the world, by operating various means of knowledge to which it has access. In the cognition of the truth of the *jagat* as *Brahmātman,* as oneself, the mind has no active role. In the cognition of objects, the mind is the operator of the *pramāṇa*, but in the cognition of oneself as *pūrṇa,* the whole, the mind is operated upon by the *pramāṇa* known as the Upanishad.

Understanding this allows us to listen differently. We do not listen analytically or critically. We listen reverentially, not to gather information, but with an intent to be transformed. We listen to lose the idea that we are the agents of knowledge. This is a different kind of listening. You relax and listen, and the resistance to the words is taken care of by the teaching methodology itself. That is why there are jokes, so that one can relax. When you laugh, you relax. The pedagogy of self-knowledge bypasses all mechanisms of rejection.

Question: The question concerns finding a guru, and while we all hope to be blessed with a personal guru, the reality is that many of us struggle in this search. How far can we go, and how much effort should we exert in finding a guru? Is it okay to study with many gurus, or should I just look for one guru?

Answer: Adi Shankara, was one of the greatest *jñānīs* and teachers of all time, and an early link in our tradition. During a time when wild animals roamed freely, he journeyed from Kerala to Madhya Pradesh to find a guru as an eight year old boy. This story illustrates that no effort is wasted–everything that one does to find a guru is worthwhile. Seeking a guru is not like searching for a sale in a mall, especially after Thanksgiving. What a way to give thanks! In America, not many people awaken at 4:00AM. But on the day of this special sale, they will go to great lengths to find the things they need, including standing in line at the front of the shops in the mall before 5:00AM. Therefore, any effort is worth it. Finding a guru is about losing one's ignorance and understanding the glory of oneself. We must acknowledge the reality of the present. Today, we are not living in Adi Shankara's time. The connection between study and freedom is not well understood. This is a big challenge for students. There is much confusion about what a guru is and how to find one.

Additionally, there is FOMO– the fear of missing out. Deciding which guru to follow can be difficult; perhaps one guru is strict, and you think you need that. Or maybe another one gives better *prasāda*, and maybe yet another guru is good at pampering. One wants everything. In this frenzy, an unsung guru that one had met and dismissed, may also be giving *prasāda*– the *mahāprasāda* of the *mahāvākya*, which totally goes unnoticed. This tendency to want everything and avoid missing out can lead to having one foot in many boats. How can you ride many boats at the same time, especially when they are all headed in different directions? If you try, you will end up falling in the water and not reaching the destination.

As a civilization, we are used to multitasking and doing many things simultaneously. We want a custom-made guru delivered to our doorstep. How is that possible? We have numerous expectations of what a guru should and should not be, but this approach does not work. Having a single guru and studying with one is becoming increasingly difficult– not because gurus are unavailable or unwilling to teach, but because people lack focus and determination. There are too many distractions vying for attention, and even if such a person sits before a guru, the guru may not feel inclined to teach. The guru might say, "You seem very busy, please carry on." The person might reply, "Oh, thank you, can I go now?" and leave. Such a person cannot gain anything from a guru.

There is no inner space to accommodate the knowledge. For these reasons, it is tempting to have a guru-buffet, where Guru A is an appetizer, Guru B is a side dish, Guru C is the main dish, and Guru D is the dessert. This creates a smorgasbord, a tasting menu of various gurus to nibble from.

This is the way of Kali Yuga, where everything is upside down. The old way of interning with one guru is on the decline because people lack the requisite focus, determination, and perseverance. Anxiety, fear of missing out, and the desire to be in a 100 places at once make it challenging. Therefore, this nibbling approach is acceptable; it is the reality for most people with a full-time job and other preoccupations. We must accept this reality. Can you go guru hopping? Having a guru, even with a buffet-psychology or the guru-hopping approach, is better than having no guru at all.

As the desire to learn increases, confusion decreases, one does settle down. The pandemic came with a blessing: gurus now come to your living room or wherever you have your computer. It is no longer gurukulam, it is Zoomkulam.

People frequently ask me in Zoom classes, "Where are you?" I say, "I am in your house, in your room." Between not studying at all and studying with many teachers, I would choose the latter. It is good to have a teacher. You have to begin somewhere, and having more gurus mean there are more blessings. We have to take it that way.

Question: I have a question about the guru and the disciple. You were saying in the old days, disciples stayed for 33 years in an ashram looking after cows. You mentioned that has changed in today's world because of Zoom. My question is how that relationship should be today? Here at Sivananda Ashram, Swami Sivanandaji died over 60 years ago. If the guru has passed away, will he still be teaching in a subtle way?

Answer: Civilization itself has undergone a change. Who has the time to take care of a cow even for 3 hours, let alone for 33 years? In contemporary times we lack focus and determination, and we want instant gratification. People want "immediate enlightenment" without needing to prepare for it. The relationship between self-growth and emotional maturity as a preparation for this knowledge is not understood.

Furthermore, people do not grasp why a guru is essential for gaining this knowledge. Earlier, it was understood, because the culture revered gurus regardless of whether one sought knowledge from them. If someone desired knowledge, they cherished the opportunity and approached the teacher for it. Now, this dynamic has shifted: everyone wants the guru to choose them, which is a form of spiritual romanticism or wishful thinking. This change is significant.

Additionally, there is a general fear of committing to gurus, ashrams, and lineages. Previously, a guru's reputation was sufficient reason to study with him or her. Now, one must Google a guru, and see if he or she is worth following. I am told that there are sites listing fraudulent gurus along with their misdeeds.

The internet is very helpful in this regard, providing guru-reviews. A guru with a one-star rating is to be avoided at all costs, as this is the lowest rating possible. People even comment that they would prefer to give zero stars if they could. All these factors contribute to our mistrust and fear of commitment, making it difficult for anyone to commit to anything.

The next part of the question is: Is it enough to commit to a guru who is no longer in the body? Is a deceased guru sufficient for gaining *ātmajñāna*? I would say yes and no. Yes, because the guru who is no longer in the body serves as an altar of surrender. While alive, the person was a *mahātman,* somebody great, and perhaps you read their works and felt, "I really want you to be my teacher. I want you to lead me." In such cases, that teacher, though no longer in the body, will bless you to find a teacher who is in the body. This is exactly how it works, driven by your sincere, burning desire to study and learn.

What needs teaching is not the subtle body—it is merely baggage and it is inert. The gross body also does not need teaching. Telling the body, "Hey, you are Brahman," makes no difference to it. The mind, too, does not need the teaching. So, what is it that needs teaching? *The ahaṅkāra* needs teaching. The "I" notion, which has mistaken itself to be finite and limited, needs the teaching. Is it possible to listen to a guru's extensive audio material and gain this knowledge? Yes, it is possible.

But my question then would be, what is wrong with a guru who is alive? What is the issue there? One might feel safe with a guru who is no longer in the body– one perhaps thinks "you cannot hurt me, you are in some other realm, you cannot disappoint me, you cannot let me down." There is a kind of safety with a guru who is no longer in the body, but this sense of safety may also indicate a latent complacency.

Vedanta requires a leap of faith and therefore, one must choose the guru properly. That is crucial. Once a proper choice is made, one can commit and this commitment brings up core issues and fears. We work with these, and through the process of dealing with our blocks, we grow.

Grace

Question: What is grace? Grace seems to be the highway to self-knowledge. We have two

kinds of pictures regarding this concept of grace. One, that we have to work hard to get grace. Or is grace a gift from God?

Answer: Let me try to answer this question gracefully! In the Christian tradition, from what I understand, grace is exactly like what you said– it is a gift from God, and it is dispensed according to God's will.

In the Hindu tradition, the understanding of grace is slightly different. We do not say it is dispensed, nor do we say we have to work hard for it. It is somewhere in the middle. It is one's own *karmaphala,* the result of actions done in the past. This part is important. I cannot gain the fruits of your actions, and you cannot have the fruits of my actions. We each keep our own fruits, as the story of Valmiki illustrates. One may have multiple desires: to be successful, to be rich, and perhaps to study Vedanta.

The desire is there, and there is a pathway for the fulfillment of that desire. One pathway is through living life, working for it, and doing what is necessary. However, sometimes, despite one's best efforts, the neighbor on the left side gets rich, and the neighbor on the right side gets famous, while one's own prayers appear to remain unanswered. Actually, the answer may be "not yet," which we often do not want to hear. Despite our efforts, if something is not coming true, it means there is a karmic impediment. We can intercede on our own behalf and pray for that impediment to be removed so that we can achieve what we desire.

Whether it is to study Vedanta, or whether it is to be rich and famous, one can pray. Prayer, in a way, is a conscious and sophisticated intercession on one's own behalf. This is to say, "Come on! Where has all my good karma from previous lives gone? O Lord! Activate them! O Goddess! Activate them and let me have the fruits of this and let me have what I want." Grace is then tapped; it is unlocked.

It is not that you must take many births. How many births have we taken already? We do not know. Therefore, we do not worry about the number of births. We do not think, "How many more births until I become a *ṛṣi*?" You do not become a sage by taking many births; you become a *ṛṣi* by knowledge, by study, by keeping the heart free to study and learn. Not burdening the heart with useless things in life like grudges, *rāga-dveṣas,* anger or jealousy is key.

In the Hindu tradition, grace is earned by *puṇya*, including prayer. It is not hard to earn grace; it is much easier to earn than money. Money comes and goes, but when grace comes, it brings with it a potential for transformation. That is how it is.

In the study of Vedanta, we talk about three kinds of grace whose blessings we need. All of them start with M in Sanskrit. It is like the M&M candy but with an extra M: M&M&M. The first M is *manuṣyatva,* a human birth. It is a big grace. Without this grace, one could be a four-legged animal grazing outside. One could be an ashram cow. One might be grazing right behind the hall where the *mahāvākya* is being taught, yet, one does not understand anything. Human life is the first act of grace, which we have already earned. We do not have to work for this. How do I know if I am a human being? Do you complain? Yes! Okay, then you are definitely a human being. So, that means the first M is already gained.

Then the next grace we pray for is called the second M, a long word– *mumukṣutva*. It simply means the desire for freedom. The desire for freedom from anything that I do not want, any sorrow, any pain, or fear. I want to be free of it. And that also is already gained. Without *mumukṣutva*, no one would be sitting in a Vedanta class. Even if you do not know the meaning of the word, you must know that you have it. You have a desire to be free of this kind of life. The daily grind: eat, sleep, wake up, go to work; eat, sleep, wake up, go to work. This is not what you want. You want to know what you are missing. You want to know how to be free of the daily grind, and the resultant sorrow and fear it brings, how to outgrow being bound to things and people that no longer serve the highest good, and how to be connected to the source. How can this oneness that you crave be achieved? This is *mumukṣutva*.

The third M is *mahāpuruṣa-saṃśraya*, which means taking refuge in a teacher. That is very important because I cannot be free without some help. I need some help to not get in my own way. Everybody needs help. However there is a peculiar phenomenon in the *jagat*. If we do not know cooking, we do not mind going to a culinary school. People do not mind doing that. If you do not know how to dance, you have no problem going to a dance instructor. If you do not know how the stock market works you will definitely approach someone who can help you to invest properly. Nowadays there are many gurus. All of them call themselves gurus– cooking guru, dance guru, music guru, stock market guru. People do not have any problem going to a stock market guru. If all else fails and you are a celebrity in Hollywood, you also need a life guru, also known as a life coach.

If a celebrity is about to have a wardrobe malfunction because they have too many mismatched clothes, what do they do? They call up the life-guru for help. The life-coach says, "Breathe, take some deep breaths." They change the tone of their voice to calm the person down during their meltdown. Then they say, "Slowly look around, is there a paper bag next to you?" "Yes." "Okay, breathe into the paper bag, a little bit of carbon dioxide is very good to clear the head of anxiety." This is a life coach. I met one in Colorado at a conference. The life coach told me all about his work coaching celebrities on how to have a good life. Six months later, I ran into him again. I asked, "Hey, how's it going?" He replied, "I am having marital difficulties." The poor life coaches also have such problems– what to do?

Even though the word guru is used for all kinds of artists, helpers, and teachers, the true meaning of the word guru is reserved for the *mahāvākya-upadeśa-kartṛ*– the one who teaches that the self non-separate from the whole, from the source of this universe. That is the traditional definition of a guru, the one who dispels ignorance and gives knowledge. *Saṃśraya* means taking refuge in such a guru. The Upanishads do not speak for themselves – the guru is the narrator of the Upanishad and the amplifying microphone of the *śāstra*, bringing it to life and making it pertinent to the contemporary milieu so that the teachings are better able to reach you.

Reading the Upanishad translations, you understand nothing. Three kinds of grace are talked about, and you have to earn these. Grace for the pursuit of knowledge and for knowing the self. It is not difficult because the first two are already gained. Only one is left.

Question: Swaminiji, I was talking with a friend who said that sometimes grace takes over. So, I wanted to know your thoughts on that statement and what it takes for a person to actually get out of the way and receive grace.

Answer: It looks like you already know the answer. Exactly what it takes is to get out of one's own way. When there is too much of oneself, there is not much room for *Īśvara*, *Bhagavān*, God to abide. Therefore, Pujya Swamiji says that the prayer of everyone on the spiritual path must be, "Let there be less and less of me. O Lord! May more and more of you abide in me as me." This prayer invites grace. Less of me means less agenda, less conflict, less fear, fewer binding desires, etc. That leaves the room for *Bhagavān*'s will to come through.

Question: What does grace mean? What can we do to earn more grace?

Answer: I will address the second part first. To earn more grace, we can pray. Grace is more easily earned than money, because when you pray, something magical happens, which seems inexplicable but actually has a clear explanation. When you pray, the free will is totally free.

In prayer, the will is truly free because your heart is not set on any specific outcome. For example, if you plan to go to a movie and if the tickets are sold out, or if the movie does not meet your expectations, you feel disappointed. But in prayer, you do not have to pray– it is a choice.

Consider someone who needs money and prays for Lakshmi to come into their lives. They could choose to do something else, like rob a bank, but they decide to pray. This choice reflects a surrender to the forces of the universe and an attempt to reverse the karma that is denying them what they need. The will is free because praying is a choice, not a necessity. Thus, grace is earned by choosing to pray and surrender.

There are only two conditions where the will is free: in praying and in reaching out actions like donating or helping someone in need–*sevā*. In *sevā*, the will is free because you need not do it, and in prayer, also, the will is free. That is why grace goes along with prayer.

Grace is an outcome of prayer because it mitigates or even neutralizes obstacles standing in the way of one's desires. We say "guru's grace" because, in the tradition, we consider the guru to be an embodiment of *Īśvara*, of God. Therefore, guru's grace and *Bhagavān*'s grace are the same. That is why sometimes the Upanishads observe that the student started to study having pleased the guru.

As a child encountering such stories, I wondered why gurus needed pleasing. Later, I understood that the teacher is already pleased; you do not have to put the teacher in a good mood. That is not the idea. Pleasing the guru means showing that you are ready to study. That is how you earn the guru's grace.

Having the guru's grace means that the teaching is easily transmitted, but if I do not have space to receive them, the teachings will boomerang back to the teacher. If I am full of myself, then there is no room for anything else. There is a story you may have heard. It is a well-known story about a university professor who went to interview a famous Zen master. The professor said, "Oh Master, I have a lot of questions to ask you." The master replied, "Okay, but we will have tea first." The professor was pleased, thinking how nice it would be to have tea with the master. The master poured tea into the professor's cup and continued pouring until the tea started to overflow and spilled on to the floor. The professor exclaimed, "Master! Master! what are you doing?" The master responded, "Your head is just like this cup right now. It is so full that there is no space for me. You say you have come to ask me questions, but you are so full of yourself that there is no place for my answers. Go, sit somewhere, clear your head, and then come back."

The spiritual aspirant's prayer should be, "Let there be less of me and more of you, O Lord! O Guru, abide in me." More of "me" means more pain, more sorrow, more questioning, more doubt, more scarcity, more complexes. When one prays for more *Īśvara* to abide in oneself, there is greater surrender and peace.

Chapter 10
MOKṢA AND NON-DUALITY

Liberation and Rebirth

Question: Is there any human being who is so brilliant or extraordinary that they are born enlightened, as mentioned in the *śāstras*, or does every person have self-ignorance at birth?

Answer: It is possible to be born enlightened, although such instances are extremely rare because the very cause of birth is self-ignorance. We have examples like sages Vāmadeva and Aṣṭāvakra in the tradition, who were born with the knowledge of the self.

There is something called *śiṣṭaprārabdha*. *Prārabdha* refers to the karma one is born with, but *śista-prārabdha* means there is a residual *prārabdha* karma, which can influence the timing of death. Consider a scenario where a *jñānin* (a person of self-knowledge) dies, dropping the body before his or her time.

For instance, if a *jñānin* was supposed to live for 70 years but due to certain lifestyle choices, like subsisting on *bhikṣā,* alms, neglecting the body, etc., they drop the body at 45. This residual *prārabdha* could result in a brief rebirth where the person is immediately self-aware and understands the nature of reality. This is possible but extremely rare.

An equally rare occurrence is someone who is almost fully enlightened but has some lingering vagueness or doubt. They may need just a bit more clarity to achieve complete understanding. This scenario is more common than being born fully enlightened.

One example that comes to mind is Aṣṭāvakra, the sage born with eight bends in his body. Aṣṭāvakra's parents were students of the Veda, and during her pregnancy, the mother was attending classes at the *gurukula*. The unborn baby was also listening. During one of the classes, the baby corrected the chanting pronunciation of his father from the womb. The father was enraged by the insolence of someone yet to be born, and cursed the baby to be born with deformities. This is one of the stories surrounding Aṣṭāvakra's life.

Consequently, he was born nearly enlightened but with eight bends, or deformities, in his body. Despite these challenges, he went on to write the *Aṣṭāvakra-Gītā*, a profound work on Vedanta.

Question: What is *pratyagātman*? Is identifying as *pratyagātman* a phase/stage for a *mumukṣu* (seeker of liberation)?

Answer: *Pratyagātman* literally means "inner-self," referring to the awareness obtaining within the body-mind-sense complex. It is the in-dweller, the truth of the observer, and is unaffected by anything happening to the body or the mind. You can say that identifying as *pratyagātman* can be considered a stage or phase for a *mumukṣu*. It is part of the journey to understanding oneself as *sarvātman,* the all-pervasive, sentient, limitless presence that dwells in everything.

Question: How does a spiritual aspirant know that self-ignorance is fully removed and that *mokṣa* is gained? Is it a sudden flash? Is it when they experience no limitations while transacting in the limited world? What is the criterion given in Vedanta for a *jīvan-mukta*?

Answer: *Mokṣa* is not an event that happens to the self. The idea that "enlightenment" is an event is fundamentally flawed. Events unfold in time, and if this were true of self-knowledge also, it implies that the self is changeable and subject to time, which it is not. This is why *mokṣa* is not something that happens to the self. *Mokṣa* does not come from somewhere, like dropping from the sky. *Mokṣa* is your nature. You are already free! The discovery of this freedom– that "I am whole," "I am limitless," "I am free of sorrow and pain"– depends on the dropping of various misconceptions and gaining clarity.

Clarity dawns slowly. Initially, there are many "aha" moments in class where one thinks, "Yippee, I think I know!" Then, three months later, one says "I thought I knew then, but now I really know." And then some more time later, "What was I thinking? Oh, that was nothing. Now, I really know." Finally, when one truly understands, they might say, "What is there to know? Brahman? I cannot say I know it; I cannot say I do not know it. It is other than the known, and other than the unknown."

The resultant clarity of self-knowledge is a process– a gradual dropping of *rāga-dveṣa*, anger, erroneous notions, pet peeves, and dysfunctional ways of interacting with others and with one's own body-mind complex. It involves shedding codependent relationships and other strong emotions. It includes processing childhood trauma and hurts and being together as a person, who is relatively cheerful, and moderate. This entire process allows the knowledge to take place because it is already you.

When you hear that you are the whole, something happens. Yes, it resonates, but the staying power might initially be weak because desires clamor for fulfillment. In the class, everything is clear, but later on, one might not be able to grasp the nuances of what was taught. This is common. The staying power of knowledge comes from well-ascertained and well-assimilated understanding, which we call self-knowledge. It is free of doubts, vagueness, and error– a process of growing clarity.

When people assimilate the teaching, they can interact with the limited world without going through cycles of elation and dejection. The *Kaṭhopaniṣad* says, *"matvā dhīro harśaśokau jahāti:"* The wise one gives up (the predilection for) elation and dejection after knowing Brahman.

Question: I have a follow-up question on this, Swaminiji. So, the ones who are liberated, do they never come back? Why do they not come back? Because they are the ones who are enlightened and can heal the world.

Answer: They have already healed the world as much as they could because they did not get liberated after death– they were already liberated while living. In their lifetime itself they would have healed and liberated numerous people. Besides, there are no duties for the ones blessed with self-knowledge, because in understanding Brahman as the truth of themselves, they have gained everything, they have accomplished the goal of life, which is to know the self.

Question: So, do they come back?

Answer: They will not come back. There is no reason for them to come back. A person once said, "I really love my guru. Can I have the same guru in the next life also?" I told him that this would be difficult to achieve as the guru would not be planning to have another life. I told him not to worry, because if his desire to know was strong, *Bhagavān* would provide a suitable guru for him in the next life also.

Liberation of humanity does not depend on one particular person. There are many liberated beings, many people who have *mokṣa*. The person you are referring to, the liberated individual, is already liberated. That is why they are called *jīvan-mukta;* they are liberated while living, not after death or after going to some *loka*. Right here in this body, one is liberated.

One is with all other people, teaching, inspiring, doing whatever one does, and then, in response to the law of karma, when the body drops at some point, there is nothing to bring them back. The gross body is unified with the gross elements; the subtle body joins the subtle elements. There is no *sañcita-karma*, no *āgāmi-karma. Prārabdha,* which gave birth to the body is also over. The cause of birth, ignorance, being resolved by knowledge, the *jñānin* has no causal body. There are no suitcases, no passport, no vehicle, and no visa for *inter-loka* travel, and no petrol of self-ignorance to fuel the return.

What will make the *jñānin* come back? There is no impetus to come back. It is not that they are decimated, gone, or disappeared. They are one with *Bhagavān*. Even while here, they were one with *Īśvara* and then after the body is gone, they are worshipped like *Īśvara*.

It is like a gold chain. Suppose someone inherits a gold chain but does not like the design, they take it to a jeweler. In India this is a common practice. You take the chain to the jeweler, who gives you the money for the gold. Then, you make a new necklace for yourself.

You cannot say the first necklace is destroyed. It has just gone back to gold. Similarly, the *jñānin* is not destroyed. The *jñānin* is very much there as an altar of worship and surrender. This is why we revere the gurus for centuries, long after they are gone. Since they do not want anything, they become an altar of wish fulfillment and surrender for those who pray to them. They fulfill your wishes, they give you whatever you want. The *Muṇḍakopaniṣad* says *"ātmajñaṃ hyarcayet bhūtikāmaḥ"*– May the who is desirous of prosperity worship the person of self-knowledge.

I must also add that in the Tibetan Buddhist tradition, they believe that the enlightened soul takes birth again. For example, a small child is brought to the ashram and shown the things belonging to the recently departed Lama. The boy will look at a cup and certain scrolls and say, "This is mine." That is how that child is chosen to be the next Lama. In our tradition, we do not have that. The *jñānin's* work on earth is done, and they then become an altar for everybody. They do not need to come back.

If you were to ask, "What about all the other ignorant people in the universe? Who will take care of them?" There will be people that this *jñānin* has taught, or other enlightened, liberated individuals who can lead them.

Advaita: Non-Duality

Question: Swaminiji, we are listening to your *Gaṇapati Upaniṣad*. We understand theoretically what self-knowledge is, but what does that mean? How do we realize it? You talked about non-duality; how do we realize that in ourselves? What would be the next steps?

Answer: You see, our orientation is like this: first, we say "Get the theory, and then we get the practice." That is how we think, but Vedanta is not like a recipe book. First, you look at the recipe book, then you buy the ingredients, and then you follow the recipe:

mix, stir, cook, and now it is ready. Vedanta is not like that because it is just telling you what you already are, even now.

There is nothing to realize. You may say, "I do not know it," or "I am in the process of knowing it." That you can say, and that is a valid point. In that case, we keep listening. This is not a one-time thing– this is a lifetime commitment. It is a long-term commitment. Let me not scare people away, especially those who are here for the first time. It is not a one-time deal, but thankfully there are resources.

You have to listen. You have to do what you are doing here. You should continue that practice at home or wherever you are. Thankfully, there is Zoom, YouTube, and all kinds of resources. You take every opportunity to sit and listen, and it wears out the ragged, jagged edges of the personality.

At first, a river stone sitting at the bottom is full of sharp edges– this is how our personality is before Vedanta. What does Vedanta do? Vedanta does exactly what the river does. Just as the river wears out the edges of the stone and makes it smooth, listening to Vedanta rounds off the personality, wearing out the strong preferences and the feeling that things must be in a certain way because the *rāga-dveṣa* say so. The belief that "this is what it should be, otherwise I cannot accept it" wears away. The feelings of "I will fall sick if I do not get my way," "I am an idiot," "I am no good," "I have to be like this only," "I have to achieve so and so to be accomplished or famous"– all these wrong perceptions wear off. The more you listen to the Upanishad teachings, the more it smooths out the personality.

When a diver goes into the Narmada river, he brings out a round, smooth oval stone, a Narmada *śivaliṅga*– it is beautiful. If a stone, which is rigid and inert, can be made into a *śivaliṅga* by being rocked by the waves in the riverbed, what can be said of a sentient human being rocked in the lap of the compassionate śruti? Even the most stubborn resistance can be worn down by the Upanishad, which is like a river of knowledge.

Question: I wanted to know if you could summarize duality and non-duality a little bit for us. I think it is an advanced topic, but just for the newly initiated people to understand a little bit, Swaminiji.

Answer: *Advaita* is neither hard nor easy to understand, but it requires a different mindset. One needs to relax and not worry about whether they are getting it. You are getting it; it is just a matter of being with it.

Vedanta, in simple terms, says that you are the most significant thing in this entire universe. You are the only self-aware entity. Everything is evident to you; you alone are self-evident. Everything in the universe depends on you to be cognized. The universe is not independent of you, the cognizing entity, the conscious entity. You are the observer; you illuminate all objects, and you yourself are self-lit. Therefore, you do not need to be illuminated. This is why you are the most significant thing in the universe.

What is this "you"? When we unpack the word "you," we do it systematically. Everything that is changing and finite is cognitively removed from the definition of "you." Is the body changing or not? Yes, and so it is gone. Bye bye, body. Is the mind changing or not? "Never mind," is all you can say about the mind. Bye bye, mind. Are the sense organs changing or not? "Huh? What? what did you say? I cannot hear...!" To the sense organs also we bid farewell. What else is there? Is the memory changing or not? You can say, "I do not remember." Are desires changing or not? Yes. All the changing entities are gone. All this is not in the equation right now. When all these are cognitively discounted, what remains is just awareness, consciousness. "I am." I am conscious of myself. That is all that remains. This is the first point.

Then how does this "I am" become evident? It becomes evident in the form of "I know." This is point number two. "I am" really means "I know." How long does this "I am" last? "I am now, I am now, I am now, I am now, I am now, I am now, I am now." For how long?

What is the length of this "now"? The length of "now" cannot be measured because "now" depends on the one who cognizes the "now."

The cognizer of the "now" has no expiration date. Thus, when one is cognizing oneself as "I am now." "Now" has no expiry date– it is *ananta*, limitless. So, "now" outlives the body, outlives the mind, outlives the senses, outlives everything. It is just always "now," which means it exists forever. Consciousness, which expresses itself as "I am" and "I know" is forever. It is the forever one seeks all the time.

> **अहमस्मि सदा भामि कदाचिन्नाहमप्रियः ।**
> **ब्रह्मैवाहमतः सिद्धं सच्चिदानन्दलक्षणम् ॥**
> ***ahamasmi sadā bhāmi kadācinnāhamapriyaḥ*** **I**
> ***brahmaiva'hamataḥ siddhaṃ saccidānanda-lakṣaṇam*** **II**
>
> I exist, and I am ever self-evident, never am I an object of distaste. Therefore I am Brahman, which is *saccidānanda*. II AM 2 II

"I am." How do you know this? Because of the shine of that knowledge, "I am." I am there forever as "me." I *bhāmi*, I shine by myself. This does not mean I am an isotope. No, it is not a radioactive shine; it is the shine of self-awareness: I know I am. And what kind of knowing is it? It is a knowing that never becomes "I do not know."

For all other objects, you can say, "I know." For example, "I know Chinese food," and you can also say, "I do not know the Greek language." But how do you know that you know? "I just know that I know." How do you know that you do not know? "I know that I do not know Greek." I met someone from Greece, and I was very curious about this. I said, "In all other parts of the world, we say 'This is Greek to me.' What do you say?" The lady said, "Oh, that is very easy. We say, 'It is Chinese to me.'" I know that I know, and I know that I do not know. The "I know" is an ontological "I know," one which can never be converted into "I do not know." This is what *sadā bhāmi* means: I am ever the same, and I always am that which never turns into "I do not know." I am that consciousness which knows itself and knows everything else.

Then the next thing he said is, *kadācin nāham apriyaḥ,* never am I unlovable. "Oh, come on," someone can say, "This is a very tall order. You do not know me. You do not know my life. I am filled with self-loathing." If someone can say that it is interesting because when the so-called self-hatred is unpacked it reveals something else.

I am not tall enough, I am not the right weight, I do not have the right complexion, the texture of my hair– i.e., if I have hair– is all wrong. In this manner one will give a whole list of things they do not like about themselves. This means that in the absence of those attributes, one is in love with oneself. One is definitely in love with oneself.

One cannot pass by a reflecting surface without taking a look, even if it is a store window and even if one does not like their looks. They will still look and say, "Oh, okay, here I am." Even if someone is 95 years old and they pass by a reflecting surface, their face may look like a road map, but still, they will turn to look. That is the love for the self. Here the self is being equated to the body because they do not know their true nature, that is all. The self is eminently lovable. Therefore, everything in the universe is lovable for the sake of the pleased self.

What does that mean? It means that certain things are lovable in their presence, like the beach is lovable; flowers, grass, trees, and mountains are all lovable when they are present around us. Unloved things, such as alligators, snakes, and cockroaches are lovable when they are far away from us. Therefore, everything is lovable, either by its presence or by its absence. This is the next point.

The author in the *Advaita Makaranda* text says, *brahma eva aham ataḥ siddham*. It is established without a doubt that I am this Brahman alone, which is just awareness, which is *ānanda*, the source of all happiness, and which is *sat*, the source of all existence.

It is understood that I am *saccidānanda*. This is something very nice to keep seeing, to keep repeating: "I am *saccidānanda*! I am *saccidānanda*!" Even when you are crying, say "I am *saccidānanda*" while wiping the tears, away. It happens to be the truth.

It is the *saccidānanda ātman* that upholds the tears. Tears come and go just like a drizzle. The *ātman*, you, is here to stay. If you are crying for two days straight, it is monsoon, that is all. It is an inner monsoon. Otherwise, it is just a little rainfall. It is the *saccidānanda* upon which this rain shower is projected. That is all. The *saccidānanda ātman* does not melt in the deluge of tears. It is totally unaffected.

The *saccidānanda ātman* is like space when it rains. Does space get wet when it rains? No. Space is unaffected by the rain. It cannot get wet. You are like space, you are the all-pervasive consciousness that is unaffected by anything.

This fact is beautifully expressed in one of the concluding verses of the eighth chapter of the *Pañcadaṣī*:

> **मायामेघो जगन्नीरं वर्षत्वेषा यथा तथा।**
> **चिदाकाशस्य नोहानिर्न वा लाभ इति स्थितिः॥**
> *māyāmegho jagannīraṃ varṣatveṣa yathā tathā*। *cidākāśasya no hānirna vā lābha iti sthitiḥ* ॥
>
> *Māyā* is the raincloud, the *jagat* is the water. Let her rain however she wants. For space-like consciousness, there is nothing to gain or lose. This is abidance in knowledge. ॥ P 8.74 ॥

Māyā is like a rain cloud, a personal rain cloud of gloom and doom born of self-ignorance. What is *jagat*? The *jagat* is the rain.

The *māyā* cloud is raining the *jagat*, including my personal *jagat* of likes, dislikes and projections. "What is this *māyā* up to right now?" wonders the ignorant one, while the person of knowledge says, "Let her rain whenever she wants, wherever she wants. Let her reign."

Is space affected by rain? Just as the space remains unaffected by rain and does not need a towel to dry itself off after being in it, so too this consciousness is not affected by the *jagat*, by anything that makes one cry. Any depression, sorrow, or fear is just a passing emotion. Every emotion must be looked upon like the weather. "This too shall pass, this too shall pass," must be our mantra.

The weather is sometimes unpredictable. Perhaps, that is why it is called "weather" because you do not know whether it is going to rain or not. But emotions are eminently predictable; that is why there is a branch of knowledge called psychology, the study of emotions. If emotions were not predictable, how could we study them?

Given a certain background, we can say that a person will have emotional hangups or trust issues. For instance, adult children of parents given to alcohol have a specific kind of personality. They will have certain emotional issues. It is not a personal issue; it becomes a syndrome common to everyone with a similar background.

Given a background of neglect, a person will have certain issues connecting to people when they grow up. It is a law. It is *Īśvara*! It is amazing, and when you look at it from that standpoint, it is no longer *my* sorrow, *my* pain. It is just the law of psychology. It is a very nice way to depersonalize it. *Īśvarize* the emotions. This is how you understand yourself. The essence of yourself, *saccidānanda*, is equated to *Īśvara*, the cause of the universe. When we say cause, that is the final point. The cause of the universe is a daunting thought.

Īśvara, OMG! so big, so powerful! Walking around the Sivananda ashram, it is very nice to see so many wood-cut murals of various *devatās* authentically painted. If one looks at these murals, one may wonder, "How can I be her? How can I be him?" The equation is not made on the obvious level of the *upādhi*, the name and form. The differences are obvious, like between a monarch and his servant. Essentially both are men, but with totally different statuses. One is the ruler, and the other is the ruled. Let us illustrate this with a story.

Once upon a time, there was a king with a rogue sentry. This sentry pretended to be a good doorkeeper, but was secretly plotting to overthrow the king. One day, seeing that everyone around was preoccupied preparing for a celebration leaving the king in his charge, the sentry threatened the king with his sword. He stuck his sword in the king's neck and said, "Quick! take off all your regalia. Give me your crown, give me your cape, give me your scepter, give me all the power symbols. Give them to me. Give me your clothes." The king protested, "What are you doing? You are supposed to be my servant."

"Shut up!" said the sentry. If you do not want to lose your head, just shut up and take off all your clothes." The king said "But I will not have any clothes to wear." The sentry replied, "Don't worry! You will wear my clothes."

It was a forcible exchange of uniforms. Now the king is dressed as the sentry, and the sentry is masquerading as the king. The sentry-turned-king, ascends the throne. He claps his hands and calls out. A lot of people gather, eager to help. "What do you want, Maharaj? Your wish is my command."

The "king" says, "Arrest that sentry! He is the most dangerous man in the whole kingdom. Just now, he was trying to capture me and overthrow the kingdom. I saved myself with great difficulty. Thank God you all came!" The poor king, in the sentry's uniform, says, "Fools, look at me. I am your king!" The sentry-turned-king then says, "Not only is he a rogue, but he is also insane. He is hallucinating about being the king. Take him away." The point here is that nobody sees the person, they see only the uniform. They see the get-up and mistake it for the person. In the same manner, on the level of the absolute, the *ātman* that is the same in all is not recognized to being subtle and due to not being an object

That is how the setup is. *Īśvara*, the monarch of the universe with a limitless *upādhi*, is a daunting phenomenon, especially from the standpoint of the *jīva*, who feels like a servant. *Īśvara* rules over the *jīva; the jīva,* therefore, is always overruled.

You make *Īśvara* take off the crown of the king of the universe, the cape of the creator of all things, and the scepter of the resolver. What is left is *saccidānanda ātman*. On the side of the *jīva*, the accoutrements of the costume in the form of the smallness, the tears, the fears, and complaints, all come off. They are all an as-though projection on the same *saccidānanda ātman,* which is absolutely free of all superimposition. When the *jagat* is gone, all these are also gone. *Īśvaratva* is gone; *jīvatva* is also gone. No *Īśvara-hood*, and no *jīva-hood* remain. The only thing that is left is *saccidānanda*. That is how the equation is made. It may take a little time to assimilate this, but it cannot be missed.

Question: How can the physical, material world be a reflection of *aham*, which means

"I"? How can it be non-separate from me when it seems completely separate?

Answer: You have the answer in the last line of your question– "It seems." The entire question hinges on that one word –it seems. It seems completely separate. Indeed, there is no question that it appears to be separate, just like when the sun sets on the west coast, it seems to be sinking into the Pacific Ocean.

Similarly, in this case, consider the situation from a different vantage point. From the perspective of the "I"– *aham*– which is deeply entangled with the body, mind, and senses, everything seems distinct from everything else. The left hand may seem ready to fight with the right hand, especially if the right hand is dominant. "Why do you get all the credit? I can do things better than you," it might argue. This potential conflict exemplifies the perceived separateness.

The Bhagavad-Gita addresses the internal conflict between the person who wants to follow dharma and the one wanting to flout it. It already seems like there are two conflicting selves within each person. One part wants to study Vedanta and seeks a teacher, while the other wants to be pampered like a baby. Are they really two different people? No.

It is a seeming reality, just like the two birds sitting on a tree. Which tree? The tree in the *Muṇḍakopaniṣad*:

> **द्वा सुपर्णा सयुजा सखाया समानं वृक्षं परिषस्वजाते।**
> **तयोरन्यः पिप्पलं स्वाद्वत्त्यनश्नन्नन्यो अभिचाकशीति॥**
> ***dvā suparṇā sayujā sakhāyā samānaṃ vṛkṣaṃ pariṣasvajāte*** **।** ***tayoranyaḥ pippalaṃ svādvattyanaśnannanyo abhicākaśīti*** **॥**
>
> Two birds with beautiful wings embrace on the same tree. One of the two eats tasty berries, while the other just observes without eating.
>
> ॥ MU. 3.1.1 ॥

There are two birds. One is very busy looking, moving, and fluttering. What does it want? It wants berries. It is, in fact, "berry" restless for them, constantly seeking the sweet ones. It is eager to eat, moving here and there, appearing to be very busy. The other bird simply shines the light. It just sits and watches, neither going anywhere nor doing anything.

How many birds are really there? One bird appears as two because of self-ignorance.

Ignorance of the sunset makes you think the sun is sinking into the ocean. Ignorance of the moon's waxing and waning phases makes you think the moon is getting smaller and bigger. When the moon is reflected in the water, a small child might think there are two moons– one in the sky and one in the water. But there is no second moon.

All things that appear to be separate need not be. Then why do they appear so? Because I mistake the point of view for the view itself. When the view is known, one can appreciate many points of view. When you know that there is only one moon, you can appreciate its reflection in a lake. The problem is when the point of view is wrongly understood as the view. That is when one's perspective is compromised by subjectivity and it needs repairing. In fact, it requires a revolution in one's thinking. This subjective view of the universe, where everything seems different from everything else, is not conducive to a happy life. Happiness lies in oneness. No one desires for things to be separate. No one wants to be isolated from others. One wishes to be one with everything. This is why one desires oneness with everything, starting from a piece of chocolate cake all the way to *Bhagavān*.

The longing for *Īśvara* is not just a simple desire; it is a yearning for oneness. This yearning drives one to the point of madness and transforms one into a *bhakta, a* devotee. This is what compels one to seek the feet of a teacher. The yearning for oneness is the desire for *brahmavidyā*. The desire for oneness has to morph into a yearning for self-knowledge.

This is crucial to understand. If there is a yearning for oneness, and everything appears separate, it might seem as if *Bhagavān*, or whoever created this system, is somewhat sadistic.

He or she, as it were, has implanted a craving for oneness in the human being, yet, everything remains separate, and that seems to be the reality. This makes no sense. Why implant such a desire, especially an uncultivated one, in a human being if there is no solution possible? If that is not sadism, then what is? Therefore, we must seek a different explanation because the idea of *Īśvara* being sadistic does not sit well in the heart.

This yearning aligns with the truth that all is already one, and I am left to discover this by dispelling self-ignorance through the study of the statements in the Upanishad. *Mahāvākyas* are the statements that reveal the oneness between the *jīva*– the helpless, hopeless, jaded, and faded individual– and *Īśvara*.

One identifies with the restless bird, recognizing oneself as a workaholic, as a *kartṛ,* a doer, and a *bhoktṛ,"* an experiencer. One is addicted to *karmaphala,* the results of action.

But is this what you truly want to be? No. You recognize yourself as the busy bird, yet you yearn to be the bird that simply is without doing anything.

In fact, the reason it seems like there are two is due to the existence of two kinds of duality. The first type is what we call objective duality.

Objective duality is *Īśvara-sṛṣṭi*; it is how the entire *jagat* is structured. From one source, you get the five elements. Then, from these, emerge various life forms– not just human beings, but countless other life forms. The number is so vast– trillions of names and forms– that counting becomes impossible. Then there is the individual, yearning for oneness and awaiting the resolution of the universe, known in Sanskrit as *pralaya*, the dissolution of the universe. Some may dream, "Oh! When will the universe resolve so I can be one with *Bhagavān*?" This never happens. Dream on, because when the universe dissolves, what are you? You will not be standing alone– you are part of the universe. The universe includes your body-mind-sense complex, which will also dissolve. In fact, this might be the first thing to go. By our reckless actions, we are already driving ourselves towards extinction, so that might indeed be the first to disappear. So, how can you enjoy this oneness if you are waiting for the universe to dissolve? That is not a feasible plan. Therefore, we need to consider plan B.

Plan B is to enjoy oneness despite the apparent duality. The objective duality, *Īśvara-sṛṣṭi*, cannot cause sorrow, strife, or fear. It is simply the way things are. Just because you see or hear something does not mean you must become sad. Yet, people often do.

This occurs because there is a second type of duality: an interface or filter between oneself and the first type of duality, *Īśvara-sṛṣṭi*. This second type is called *jīva-sṛṣṭi*. It is our own projection, a filter through which we view the universe, starting with our body-mind-sense complex. Due to self-ignorance, this subjective filter distorts our perception. It is a filter that can drive one to despair.

What are the ingredients of this filter? They are early hurts, pains, fears, and sorrows. The first kind, *Īśvara's* duality, will not go away. Why? Because *Īśvara* created it, not you. It remains as long as the *jagat*, the universe, exists.

The second kind of duality is created by oneself, under the influence of two factors: self-ignorance and its offspring, misperception– a subjective view. Since this second type of duality is self-manufactured, there is hope for its retraction in the light of self-knowledge. It is like fog dissipating with the rising sun. Similarly, the rising sun of knowledge and compassion within the heart disperses the fog of subjectivity, known as *prātibhāsika*. This allows you to see the universe as *Īśvara* has made it, not as you perceive it to be.

Now, we are dealing with only one kind of duality– the objective duality. It cannot cause sorrow because it simply is. It is not out to harm you. Every person in the universe is not out to get you. Your body is not out to get you. Your mind is not out to get you. Even if there are challenges within one's body or mind, when viewed through the lens that everything is *Īśvara*'s order, a pattern emerges.

It is no longer "my" mind, "my" depression, "my" anger, "my" hopelessness, "my" sickness. Whose hopelessness is it then? It is part of the universal law. It belongs to the vast psychological order. Given a specific background– let us say, for example, one of neglect or abuse– one will have to deal with abandonment issues in adulthood.

I saw a striking cartoon posted on someone's office door. It depicted a huge auditorium. Above the stage was a large banner that read: "First Annual Convention of Adult Children of Normal Parents." The auditorium had everything: balloons, water glasses, and little notepads for the speakers. The only things missing were the speakers and the audience: the room was completely empty. This illustrates how it is. No one can have "normal parents"; one has to emotionally grow to understand that whatever parents one has are perfectly "normal," when the psychological and karmic orders of *Īśvara* are taken into account.

When you *Īśvarize* your background, you shift elements from the domain of *jīva-sṛṣṭi* to *Īśvara-sṛṣṭi*. You "*Īśvarize*" everything. Consider your own mind, which might feel heavy at times: Why do I get angry? Why am I inauthentic at times? Why do not I love myself? What is wrong with me? Now, imagine 8 billion people in the universe asking these same questions simultaneously. That is when you know that it is not personal.

When you observe the background and realize it could not be any other way and understand that you have the free will to override it. The enmeshment with the mind or an ailing body immediately starts to dissolve, allowing you to become objective. This is the first step. We should aim to live within one *sṛṣṭi,* not two. Our perspective should recognize only *Īśvara-sṛṣṭi*, *Īśvara's* creation. By retracting our own subjective creation and withdrawing it prayerfully, we are only left with only *Īśvara's* creation, in which we can participate playfully. If there is pain, we address it; whatever the issue, we take care of it. Step one is to withdraw from *prātibhāsika*, subjective, personal duality. Step two is to progress to the understanding that everything is one. Despite apparent differences, the oneness shines. This is called *sarvātmabhāva*.

That leads me to the second question. The questioner asks a very practical question: Is *sarvātmabhāva* a practical way to lead one's life? Seeing everything as one– can it be applied in everyday life, or is it only for those sitting in the Himalayas who do not interact with others? Is it for those who are unmarried and do not have family obligations? They do not need to navigate the delicate social dance of negotiating with people and managing relationships. Maybe it is for those few people, the *avadhūtas*, saintly individuals who can afford to enter a trance, regardless of who is around and what is happening.

But is *sarvātmabhāva* meant for all of us? For those who have places to go, people to see, goals to achieve– is this oneness for everyone? I If you are in the world, you definitely need *sarvātmabhāva*. In the beginning, we see everything as *Bhagavān*. Seeing everything as "I" might seem a bit distant but recognizing that everything is *Bhagavān* and that I am non-separate from *Bhagavān* is feasible. It is achievable.

This requires being comfortable with the "I" that is consciousness. This "I" must override the "I" that is enmeshed dysfunctionally with the universe and the body-mind-sense complex. That is what it takes.

Chapter 11
VEDANTA AND PSYCHOLOGY

Guilt and Free Will

Question: I am going through something that I have experienced all my life. Every day, I feel guilt and responsibility towards others. I need help with this. I am new to this practice and wonder if the conversation about grace and the three Ms, particularly *mumukṣutva*, touches on free will. Is the release of guilt and the feeling of responsibility for others really my choice?

Answer: Yes, releasing guilt is a choice. You can make the choice, but as guilt is habitual, it will take a little while to wear out its welcome in the light of the awareness that the *ātman* is naturally free of guilt and hurt. The habit will eventually go away. There is a *mantra* of self-affirmation: "I am enough, I do enough." Keep repeating this *mantra*. "I am of total value. If all I do from here to the rest of my days is to just sit and breathe, I am still valuable. I am enough."

This discernment is very healthy, and I applaud you for it. I commend you because recognizing that there is a pattern here, a leakage of energy, is important. There is a pattern of trying to help excessively. It is okay to need to help, but sometimes, we are over-involved in situations because we do not trust that things will be taken care of.

One lady came to see me and said, "I am in a terrible quandary. My teenage children are having exams, my husband cannot even boil water– he is inept at everything– and my father is sick. I have to go to India to take care of him, but I do not know how the family will manage without me for two weeks." I said, "They will be okay, you can go." After the lady left, the husband and the teenagers also wanted to meet me privately. They said, "We need a break from her. Please make her go to India."

We often think that we are indispensable, and without us, everything will fall apart. This is an overdose of *kartṛtva*, doer-ship, which can foster a sense of over-responsibility, leading to the thought that without us, nothing will function. But things do run, and in fact, they thrive not because of us, but in spite of us. Trust that *Bhagavān* will take care. Say a prayer and just believe it will happen.

If you are not there or you miss a phone call from someone in need, they will not just sit there waiting for you. They will call ten other people and get the help they need. This is what we should tell ourselves to let things be carried on. There is great grace in that– it is an act of self-grace. Allowing myself to be in a position of teachability and receptivity is the ultimate grace. It is called *ātma-anugraha,* self-grace.

Question: I was raised Catholic, and I understand that the Bible suggests our days have been predestined. God has already laid out the foundation for our life in a certain capacity. I am not sure about your tradition, but it seems to have a similar idea– that certain things are already destined for us to accomplish and complete. So, my question is about free will versus fate and destiny. Which

is stronger? What is the point of having free will if everything is already predestined?

Answer: This is an all-time favorite topic. I was wondering how we went so far into the satsang without a single question on fate versus free-will. What you call as destiny, we say is karma. Here, karma refers not to action but to the results of action. The same word is used for action and results of action, so we are actually referring to *karmaphala*, the fruits of action from deeds done either in this life or in other lives.

For example, if I am enjoying a comfortable situation– like right now; I am enjoying a wonderful time with you all– it is my good karma. The *śāstra* says that the cause of this would be some action in the past that was in tandem with dharma. This is what we say is *puṇya*, good karma. In the past life if I was a follower of dharma, then I must have made a choice to do that. Choice involves free will. Therefore, what is generally known as fate, we call it *prārabdha,* the karma that one has to undergo in this life. *Prārabdha* is the result of the free will used in the past lives.

Therefore, we can take everything as free will because the good that was done in the previous life also came from free will. I chose to do something, and now I am reaping the benefits of that.

You can say everything is free will, regardless of whether the free will was exercised in this life or another life, it does not matter. It is all free will; or you can say it is all *Bhagavān* who is the architect of both the free will and the one who gives the fruits of karma.

The fruits of karma are not literal and come in various shades, sometimes with a touch of humor. If person A took something from person B, it is not that person A will have something taken away from them. It is not so literal; it is much more creative. Whatever you have done comes back, but how it comes back or when it comes back, we say, is in the hands of *Īśvara*, who decides or manifests as the law of karma. That law decides how one is going to get it. Are we here because we were destined to be here?

Did we choose to be here at this time? Obviously, you had to make a booking at the ashram to come here. So, were you supposed to make that booking? This is a very good question, and we could ponder it endlessly. Lord Krishna in the fourth chapter of the Bhagavad-Gita sums it up by saying the ways of karma are dense. We do not fully comprehend them.

Life is not predestined because otherwise, we would not have free will. We are choosing in every situation. For instance, if someone says something unkind, I have a choice: I can tell them off and be equally unkind, or I can give them a lecture on karma, making myself feel superior by giving them a "spiritual" lesson. Or, I can just acknowledge they must be having a bad day and walk away from the situation gracefully, knowing that saying anything at this time can worsen the situation. These choices indicate free will.

If I chose to be twice as unkind and tell them off, I cannot blame that on *Bhagavān* and say I was destined to do that. It is a nice excuse, but that does not work because there were at least two other options, and likely a few more. So, either we say everything is free will and take responsibility for our actions, or we say everything is *Bhagavān* and live in a spirit of surrender like a *sādhu*. It is your choice. Or, is it?

Question: Swaminiji how would you clear **the guilt you might feel if you did not take a phone call and something terrible happened as a result of that?**

Answer: This is an important question. If you did not take the phone call, there must have been a reason, and if something terrible happened, you can forgive yourself. The circumstances of not having taken the phone call– perhaps you were busy– can lessen the guilt. If you thought the person was just badgering you and deliberately did not take the call, and then something terrible happened, the guilt would be more. You have to forgive yourself and say, "I have done the best I can, and I did the best I could," and mean that. Embrace the part of you that cannot look at itself and forgive yourself completely. In that forgiveness, there is great liberation.

After forgiving yourself, consider the karmic order. There is a karmic intelligence, and perhaps you were not meant to take that phone call. For example, if someone goes to the hospital for surgery and, despite the best efforts of the doctors, the person loses their life, there could be some human error. But why that particular day, that particular surgeon, or that particular patient? It is all karmic.

The karma of the surgeon may include being suspended from the hospital, while the karma of the patient includes the completion of life's journey. The karma of others involved, such as the hospital that may be sued by the relatives of the patient, is also part of a larger intelligence beyond our understanding. When we look at it this way, there is no guilt. Guilt is also part of that larger order. Seeing it like that makes it much bigger, and the guilt becomes just a small emotion.

Dreams

Question: I am interested in what you said the other night about dreams, specifically that I can enter any aspect of my dream and

become it. Could you please explore this further?

Answer: Yes, you are everything. You are sentient, and everything is being upheld entirely by you. The suitcase is not separate from you, but you are not the suitcase. Everything is *ātman*. *Ātman* means "I." For the *ātman* to be everything, it cannot be any one thing.

A chain is gold, a ring is gold, a bangle is gold, a nose-stud is gold, and an earring is gold. But can you say gold is a chain? No. Can you say gold is a nose stud? No. Similarly, everything is non-separate from me, and I am not any one thing.

Question: This morning we spoke about dreams and said that we should let them go. But I just had a question. Do dreams mean anything, and does the time of the dream mean anything?

Answer: Carl Jung, the famous psychologist, said that every dream is an unopened letter. The problem is that often we do not know how to open it. Jung wrote a comprehensive book on signs and symbols and their meanings. Having studied dreams in depth, he was like a *ṛṣi* with his extensive knowledge. He suggested that certain dreams could reflect parts of the unconscious mind. However, cultural symbols also play a role. For instance, in Indian culture, certain dreams are considered auspicious because they are culturally associated with auspiciousness.

Most of the time, we do not have the opportunity to work with our dreams. We must be careful not to make dreams more real than waking reality, as that can lead to confusion. It is best to observe dreams and interpret them cautiously. For example, if you dream of being chased, it could signify fear. Consider what this fear might be– perhaps a looming deadline. Once you have understood it, absorb the insight and let it go.

Some dreams are like dead letters; you cannot decode them, so you let them go. It is said that dreams occurring around four o'clock in the morning are often more lucid. Lucid dreaming is possible just before you open your eyes. These dreams can sometimes be prophetic or reveal something about yourself. However, they are challenging to decode unless one has studied Jungian psychology, which is a vast compendium of knowledge. When you gain a particular insight from a dream, you can thank *Bhagavān* and then let it go. If a dream is prophetic and you foresee something happening, you can appreciate that knowledge.

Question: My question is about self-forgiveness.
I have forgiven others a lot for trauma and letting things go, but there are things for which I have not forgiven myself. What should I say to that? And then, question two is about my family. We have dreams that serve as premonitions of things to come. What should we do with dreams that are foreboding in nature? For instance, my sister and I both dreamt about my dad dying. We called and checked on him, and he was fine on Wednesday, but that Saturday, he died. I recognize the serenity prayer about accepting things we cannot change and

having the will to change what we can. However, when we know something is going to happen but cannot change it, what do we do with that? Those are my two questions.

Answer: Dreaming is a gift. Some people experience lucid dreaming, which provides information. Why is it given? Only God knows; we do not know the reason. In a way, it is a blessing, but if you do not understand why it is given, it becomes a difficult gift because you spend the rest of the time feeling anxious about it. That is the problem. So, you convert it to prayer. You say, "I do not know why, oh Lord! Oh Goddess! you have shown us this. I do not know why, and if I am supposed to prevent something or help somebody, please show me the way." You pray. Additionally, if you know something is happening and it is foreboding, it is also time to make amends with that person. Use the time to make amends. If no amends are needed, then spend quality time to say goodbye. This is how you can fruitfully use the message or the encounter.

Self-forgiveness is very important because, really, forgiving others is easier than forgiving oneself. One is often hard on oneself because our inner child can be like a police with a whistle– an inner cop who is very critical. This leads to self-flagellation, self-loathing, self-critique, and self-judgment. To address this, mentally visualize taking away the whistle from the inner cop and replacing it with a pacifier. Whenever it says, "Wrong things are happening! You are doing this! You are doing that," give the baby cop a big hug. For many lifetimes, it has been used to being critical. With the continued assimilation of Vedanta, all these negative messages will eventually drop.

Ego and Praise

Question: I have a question about saying "no." I have difficulty saying no. I do not feel guilty, but I find that I use excuses because I am overwhelmed. How does one go about saying no and still come out looking good?

Answer: There is the rub, you see. We want to look our very best at all times. When you say no, a lot of people may react negatively. They might think, "How dare you say no? I do not like hearing it. You are the worst person on earth." These thoughts come up. One worries that if one says no, one might not be a very popular person. It is like being the person who fines a car parked in the wrong place or gives a ticket for cars with expired meters. The ticketing person is not at all popular. We greet that person the same way we greet someone who says no because everyone wants to hear the word "yes."

If you are in a place to give something that someone wants, and you refuse, for whatever reason, there is some discomfort. Therefore, we have to allow ourselves the space to feel uncomfortable when we say no and to embrace that discomfort. We have to be able to develop healthy boundaries and saying no is a salient part of that exercise.

The Vedas say, "*Satyaṃ brūyāt, priyaṃ brūyāt*," which means that one must speak the truth softly, gently, and lovingly. It is easier if we are not looking for a particular outcome, but we often want everyone to be happy while also wanting to say no. That is difficult.

So, we speak the truth but speak it nicely and lovingly. If there is something difficult to say or hear, sometimes it is better not to say it at all.

There are many ways of refusing a request that is inappropriate for you. There is body language. Perhaps one can say that one is busy right now, but would be able do the requested task later. Perhaps one might offer the other person a few other options for fulfilling their needs. These are some other options.

Question: Swaminiji, I have a question about when we receive praise or compliments. How do we not let that inflate our ego and identify with it?

Answer: This is a very good question. In India, we have a nice formula for such situations. No matter how high the praise, people will consciously deflect ownership of the praise by attributing the object of the praise to a higher power. For example, if you go to someone's house and praise their home, saying, "What a lovely house! You have kept it so nicely," they will respond, "This is the grace of God." If you praise someone's cooking, they might say, "This is the grace of God and my mother who taught me." If you compliment someone's chanting of the Vedas, they will say, "It is the guru's grace." Internally, they may feel happy and appreciated, but outwardly, they attribute the praise to God, the guru, or elders. The overt deflection prevents one from internalizing the praise, where the *ahaṅkāra* takes itself to be the recipient of the praise. Even if this practice initially starts as lip service, the spirit of seeing everything as given and of attributing all our talents to *Īśvara* eventually sinks in, helping one align with the reality. This practice helps prevent praise from affecting the psyche. However, we cannot do the same with criticism. If someone criticizes me, I cannot deflect it by saying I am like this because of the guru or elders. In that case, we must take full responsibility and be accountable for our temperament and actions.

Question: Swaminiji, with this question and the earlier discussions we have had, when someone says your dog looks nice or your

house looks nice, and you say thank you, are you saying that we need to find a balance unto whom we attribute the complement?

Answer: That was a joke to illustrate the misidentification of oneself as the body-mind-complex. The identification with *anātman*, the not-I, is so complete that if you praise the dog, the owner says thank you. If you tell a person, "nice T-shirt," the wearer of the T-shirt takes ownership of the compliment. Certain things in life are no doubt funny, but behind the mirth there is an important lesson of giving up agency and recognizing everything in the universe as God-given. Even if someone praises the dog, you can say that it is God's grace. There is nothing wrong.

Question: **I want to go back to the *yogin*'s question about having the ability to ignore or handle criticism. If we could take that one step further– if that criticism were an accusation or slander and they got kicked out of the ashram, then what happens?**

Answer: They will be fine wherever they are. Wherever they are, that is the ashram. The heart is the ashram. One learns to be at home with oneself.

Question: So they should not say anything to try to get back?

There is no should or should-not. If we are talking about a *yogin*, we are discussing a *yogin's* response here. If the person is a *yogin*, they will understand that this place is not for them. They are like a bird; if another aggressive bird pecks it out of the nest, it will simply fly somewhere else and make another nest. It will not say, "I am going to sue you. Here are the legal papers," or "I belong here." They are like birds, ever free.

This inner freedom means knowing that no matter what happens, I am okay. If someone thinks that I have done something which I have not done and says, "You cannot stay here," then where will I go? I may not know initially, but the chances are that once I leave, a series of events will intervene, and it might turn out to be the best thing that I was not in this place. It always works out because a higher intelligence is operating, and we grow into surrendering to *Īśvara's* order, no matter how it expresses itself.

Doership

Question: **In this context, I would like you to elaborate a little bit about the teaching "I am not the doer."**

Answer: That I am not the doer is correct. I grow to identify as the limitless consciousness which upholds the status of the doer in me, which manifests as the doer, but is not the doer. Why? because consciousness is limitless. It lends its presence to various statuses, such as *kartṛ*, *bhoktṛ, pramātr*, doer, experiencer, knower, etc., without "becoming" anyone of them. Pujya Swamiji would put it thus: "The doer is me, but I am not the doer."

Doing happens because of me, but I am not the agent of action. When I identify as the *kartṛ,* the agent of action, misery ensues almost immediately. If you want a recipe for instant depression, like instant coffee, say, "I have done this. I do so much everyday." From this thought, it is a short hop to the next thought, "Even though I do so much nobody gives anything back!"– see, depression is already setting in. Depression, sorrow, confusion, anger, and resentment are all rooted in the misapprehension of oneself as an agent of action.

The truth is that you are the actionless *ātman*. Because we are addicted to action, one has to repeat: "I am the actionless *ātman*. I am the limitless consciousness, which does not do anything, and which is not affected by other people's actions." Both are equally important to understand: I am neither the doer; nor I am done-in by other people's actions. I am totally free of guilt and hurt.

Guilt is an offshoot of depression, meaning you say, *kimahaṃ sādhu nākaravam*, which means, "Why did I not do the right thing?" Or, *kimahaṃ pāpam akaravam*, meaning, "Why did I do the wrong thing?" This becomes a regret. If I identify as the doer, then I am subject to guilt. If I identify as being affected by other people's actions– their omissions and commissions– it leads to hurt. One's own omissions and commissions lead to guilt and other people's omissions and commissions towards one lead to hurt. Therefore, you give up the doer-ship entirely.

How to give up doer-ship? We can recognize, *Bhagavān* as the doer, and oneself as a *nimitta*, an instrument. In the Bible also there is a prayer, O Lord, make me an instrument of your will." That is the way to start. With consistent exposure to the teachings of Vedanta, the doing becomes much simpler and does not become your undoing.

Question: Is it more habituation?

Answer: It is not just a habit; behind the habit is ignorance. Both need to be addressed. However, if one has the knowledge of the *ātman*, and yet doer-ship occasionally rears its head, one has to do spend time in contemplation.

Question: If somebody has ill will towards you or is doing bad things to you and says he is not the doer, what happens?

Answer: This is a very good point. If someone has read the Gita and then commits homicide, they might get up on the stand and plead not guilty, by virtue of being *akartṛ*, a non-doer of action. This is not something that can be done. Claiming non-doer-ship is not meant for people who do not follow dharma. This teaching is for those who are committed to righteous actions, who are ethical, who speak the truth, and who want to live in truth. At the end of many Upanishads, there is a saying: Do not give this knowledge to anyone who is not committed to a life of righteous living. Otherwise, disaster will ensue.

Question: My question is about doer-ship and enjoyer-ship. You mentioned we have these two in the waking state. I understand we need to relinquish both, but what are the steps in doing so? If I give up doer-ship but still enjoy things in life, it does not seem correct. Do we need to let go of one first and then the other, or should they be dropped simultaneously?

Answer: Both doer-ship and enjoyer-ship are equally problematic. Identifying as an agent of action leads to guilt because one constantly feels that one is not doing enough, or not doing it the right way, resulting in regret. If one identifies as an experiencer as one's sole identity, hurt ensues because one becomes dependent on others' actions or inactions for one's sense of well-being. Guilt arises from my own omissions and commissions, while hurt results from others' acts of omissions and commissions towards oneself. Guilt sounds like, "Why did I do this? Why did not I do that? How could I have been so stupid?" Hurt sounds like, "Why did they do this? Why did not they remember my birthday? Why did not they bring me a gift?" The good thing is that if you drop one, the other also drops because they are mutually interdependent. There is no formula for which one to drop first; it is like the tree and seed. Each one is the cause of the other.

Joy, Sorrow, and Mental Health

Question: How can you find joy despite all that is happening in my life? How can you see the hand of *Īśvara* in all the things that are happening?

Answer: Seeing the hand of *Īśvara* is not hard. Just think of how the entire world got shut down for nearly a year during the pandemic? Think about it. How is it possible for us to halt global travel and other activities? During the pandemic, all we could do was engage in small gestures like banging pots and pans in appreciation of medical personnel and essential workers who risked their lives for us. That became something to look forward to everyday because there were no other group activities possible.

Why does one person get sick while another, who was in close contact, remain healthy? We do not know. All the things we do not understand are manifestations of *Īśvara*. When we say, "I do not know," we are acknowledging the presence of *Īśvara*. The first part of your question is about finding joy.

This, too, is not difficult. It takes very little to laugh. People who study such things say that when you smile or laugh, you use 18 facial muscles, whereas to frown or scowl, it takes 43 muscles. So one natural way to postpone signs of aging in the form of wrinkles is to laugh more.

In India and some other Asian countries, there are groups known as "haha therapy" or laughing therapy groups. You often see them in parks. During my morning walks, I notice these groups standing around, laughing heartily for no apparent reason. There is no joke being told, yet people are laughing loudly.

Pujya Swamiji demonstrated that it is possible to laugh without even telling a joke. Here is how he explained it: One day in class, Swamiji told a joke, and everyone laughed. However, one person did not understand the joke. For a whole week, this person thought about it, trying to figure it out. Finally, he approached Swamiji and said, "I have been thinking and thinking about this joke. I did not get it the first time, but now, I think I understand." He managed to say this while he was laughing very hard.

Swamiji then asked him to explain what he thought the joke was and what he understood. When the man explained, Swamiji laughed out loud, because the man had completely missed the point. Hearing Pujya Swamiji tell this, everyone else laughed as well. What was the joke? Even to this day no one knows, but we have had four rounds of laughter already: the first laughter was in the class, when Swamiji told the original joke, the next laughter happened when the man thought he had understood the joke, the third laughter happened when Swamiji laughed at his misunderstanding. And now, in retelling this entire saga, we are all laughing again. Therefore, there were four bouts of laughter without an actual joke being told. This shows that you do not need a joke to laugh. Laughter is natural– it is intrinsic to us.

Sometimes it gets challenging, especially with the "eclipse" we keep discussing in class. Lord Krishna says, *ajñānenāvṛtam jñānam tena muhyanti jantavaḥ*. Since the knowledge of the *ātman* is as-though covered by ignorance, beings are deluded because they do not understand that the *ātman* is untouched by *puṇya-pāpa*, and consequently sorrow.

What can we do to maintain a certain lightness of being? One thing is to ensure that we can laugh at ourselves. This is invaluable. Each time you make a mistake, instead of being harsh on yourself, just laugh and say, "I am so funny. What is wrong with me? Here I go again."

When we can laugh at yourself, it becomes less painful when others laugh at us. You do not worry as much about other people's judgments because you are already comfortable laughing at yourself, relatively comfortable with who you are.

We cultivate an attitude of gratitude. We are grateful for whatever is present. Whatever we have been given everyday is *bhagavat-prasāda*– a gift from *Bhagavān*. If its hard to identify things to be grateful for, we have to look a little closer. We can start by celebrating and finding joy in the small things. As you do this, the troubles that seem overwhelming will begin to fade away. They will just recede.

Question: **In this world currently, there are many mental health issues. How can we manage and prevent them? Does Vedanta have a solution for mental illness? If not, how can we help people who struggle with mental illness?**

Answer: The core issue is a feeling of alienation– a sense of disconnect from oneself, from others, and from *Īśvara*. Addressing this disconnect is crucial.

For mild anxiety or neurosis, we need to focus on reconnecting with ourselves, our work, our communities, and with *Īśvara*. However, for moderate to severe anxiety or depression, medical consultation and treatment is necessary. These conditions often involve chemical imbalances that require professional treatment to manage the condition effectively. Vedanta alone cannot help as one needs to have a sound mind to appreciate the truth of oneself.

For common, garden-variety, neurosis we

need to address it from the perspective of alienation. If the person is willing and able, the quickest way to overcome this is through *bhakti*. Even if they claim not to be a devotee or resist the idea, you can still introduce them to *bhajans*. They can listen to calming music available on platforms like YouTube, in any language or from any culture.

Creating a relationship with an altar or a place of surrender is also crucial. Having a personal space at home where they can connect with something meaningful can greatly help in fostering a sense of connection. This is very important for their well-being.

Other practices that help include journaling, *yoga*, and therapy. These activities promote self-love and help one feel connected. Alongside *bhakti*, another effective way to address feelings of alienation is through *sevā*.

Every community has opportunities for service. Homeless shelters, soup kitchens, women's shelters, and youth clubs all need volunteers. Even if you are not living near a *gurukula*, you can find many ways to help in your own neighborhood.

Volunteering services for an hour or two, regularly contributes to discovering the presence of something larger than oneself, and one's own problems. This can significantly reduce feelings of loneliness and instability. *Sevā* can help one have a very sane and fulfilling life.

Question: Can you be content in yourself without overtly laughing and expressing happiness? How do you overcome sorrow? You are often told to look at someone who is going through worse than you, but that seems to be only a temporary solution. I would like to have your opinion.

Answer: These are wonderful questions. The person of self-knowledge is often compared to an ocean. Sometimes the ocean roars and crashes against the rocks making a lot of noise, especially during a full moon when the tides are high. On other days, it is tranquil and still. Regardless, the ocean is always full, *pūrṇa*. A person of knowledge is *pūrṇa,* and *embodies the same fullness of the ocean. At* times, a *jñānin* may laugh exuberantly, like a roaring ocean. At other times, the person may be quiet and serene, reflecting the ocean's calm.

It is not about whether you are laughing or being silent– it is the fullness that matters. Sometimes this fullness expresses itself through laughter, and sometimes through quietude.

The second part of the question touches on a common way people try to console each other. For instance, someone might say, "You feel bad because you have a sprain in your foot? At least you have a foot. Look at the person who has no legs at all." However, this perspective is limited in scope. It only works when we encounter people less fortunate than ourselves. What to do when one encounters a person who has both legs and is driving a BMW? How to reconcile to our lot then?

Relying on positive thinking alone may not help. Many people attend workshops on positive thinking, but the ones who truly benefit from them are the leaders of these workshops. Their self-esteem increases exponentially as they profit from offering them. Overcoming dissatisfaction with one's life cannot be achieved by merely comparing oneself to those who have less. This approach is just a temporary fix, like putting a bandaid on a deeper problem.

Introspection and self-knowledge are required for discovering true contentment. One can ask oneself: Why am I discontent? Why do I feel I lack something? What is missing in my life, and why does it trouble me so much? This kind of self-inquiry is essential for addressing the root of the discontent.

One can make a list. On one side of the page, one can put down all the things one has– not in comparison to others, but whatever it is one has. On the other side, one can write down all that one feels one does not have. On any given day, you will find that what you have far outweighs what you lack. This exercise helps us grow by shifting our focus.

Discontentment is often like an eclipse overshadowing the self. Pain, sorrow, fear, guilt, and hurt are projections that obscure our true nature, much like how the sun is covered by fog. Recognizing and addressing these projections is crucial for personal growth.

If I remain in the place of the *sākṣin*, the witness, I can observe my projections. If I get caught up in the projections, it means I am too close to them or have identified with them. Therefore, we take a step back. Instead of saying, "I am sad," one can say, "I am observing that I am sad." Even if others think you talk strangely, it is okay. You can respond, by saying, "Now, I am observing you saying that I am weird." When we frequently repeat something, it gains momentum and we start to live in that reality– *yadbhāvitam tadbhavati.*

This way, you maintain a sense of *asaṅgatva*, remain uninvolved, and manage the emotions effectively. For example, instead of saying, "I feel guilty," we say, "I notice that some guilt is bubbling up." Then you can tell the guilt to "bubble down," because you are in charge.

Similarly, instead of saying, "I feel hurt by what the other person did," one can say, "I am noticing some hurt feelings." It is like walking past a building and noticing a new crack. You might think, "I walked by this building yesterday and do not remember this crack. Now it has a crack. Hmmm, this is interesting." If the building is yours, you might feel more attached to the crack. But consciously dis-identifying from such ownership of the body and mind helps.

It is important to be aware of how we think and how we talk, both to ourselves and others. It shapes our reality and our experiences.
There is a common concern I hear from many professionals who say they avoid Vedanta classes because they fear becoming too content. They wonder, "If I become happy and fulfilled, who will run my company? If all people in the world get *mokṣa*, how will there be progress in the world?"

But what kind of progress are we talking about? Everyone is rushing around all the time during the day and doomscrolling on their devices at night when they cannot sleep. The next morning, one wakes up in a rush, with the heart racing, thinking, "Oh my God, what day is it? What do I have to do today?" This constant state of anxiety and urgency is not true progress.

Then you "jump into the shower"– although, no Hindu should jump into the shower. I will explain why in a moment. Next, "you grab a bite to eat" and "rush out the door." You do not drive; you "hit the road," and immediately "kill the presentation" that you had to give.

After work, you "beat the traffic" on the way home. Dinner is something hurriedly "thrown together," or if you are a young adult, as someone told me, you "just nuked it." Finally, you "crash" into bed, exhausted. Life these days is led by violent metaphors. Is this progress? When we are utterly disconnected from our body, our mind, and our senses, how can we call this as progress?

While the Buddhist tradition is often credited with the cultivation of mindfulness, especially in practices like Zen, it is important to note that mindfulness is also deeply embedded in Vedanta. Zen, with its emphasis on being fully present, is very similar to Vedanta.

There is a standing joke that illustrates this: if there is a sudden noise of a wild animal roaring behind the person, most people immediately run away, but the Zen master will take a deep breath and slowly turn the head around to see what is happening. This calm, deliberate response is very much aligned with the principles of Vedanta.

Vedanta teaches mindfulness through the first portion of the Vedas, which focuses on how to live and be in the world in the present. This ancient wisdom outlines the path to living a mindful and balanced life by converting even the most mundane actions into acts of prayer.

We are told to look at our hands, first thing upon waking. Hands are organs of action, through which we express ourselves in the world. Therefore you visualize the goddess of prosperity, Lakshmi, at your fingertips. With Lakshmi present at the fingertips, how can anything you do go wrong?

At the base of your fingers is Saraswati, the goddess of knowledge, providing wisdom and guidance. On your palms is Govinda, another name for *Īśvara*, symbolizing the one discovered in the words of Vedanta. You start your day by invoking in the hands the presence of Lakshmi, Saraswati, and Govinda. Next, we gently place our feet on the ground, touching Mother Earth, and offer a silent prayer: "May I not be a burden to you today. May I tread carefully."

It is recommended that one does not jump into the shower. Instead, consider filling a bucket with water and pouring it over oneself. The idea here is what you do to *Bhagavān*, you do to yourself. This tradition is the reason why, when elderly relatives come to visit the US from India, they often ask, "Where is the bucket?" when shown the bathroom. They feel that bathing is incomplete without it because there is a prayerful aspect to using the bucket for bathing.

> **गङ्गे च यमुने चैव गोदावरी सरस्वति ।**
> **नर्मदे सिन्धु कावेरी जलेऽस्मिन्सन्निधिं कुरु ॥**
> ***gaṅge ca yamune caiva godāvari sarasvati ।***
> ***narmade sindhu kāveri jale'smin sannidhiṃ kuru ॥***

O Ganga, O Yamuna, O Godavari, O Saraswati, O Narmada, O Sindhu, and O Kaveri, make your presence (felt) in this body of water.

We can modify the mantra *to* say, *"asmin* bucket-*jale sannidhiṃ kuru"* When you use a bucket for bathing, you can recite this prayer: "May all the holy rivers of India be present in this bucket of water." This invocation brings the sacredness of these rivers into your bath, making you feel refreshed, as if you have undertaken an actual pilgrimage.

After bathing, we apply holy ash, sandalwood paste on the forehead. This acknowledges the energy center of the third eye as the dwelling place of *Īśvara*, whom we seek to discover as the truth of the self.

One should never "grab a bite to eat." Eating is a form of worship, it is inner-*yajña*. The digestive fire is *Īśvara*. In the 15th chapter of the Bhagavad-Gita, Krishna declares:

अहं वैश्वानरो भूत्वा प्राणिनां देहमाश्रितः ।
प्राणापानसमायुक्तः पचाम्यन्नं चतुर्विधम् ॥

ahaṃ vaiśvānaro bhūtvā prāṇināṃ dehamāśritaḥ I
prāṇāpānasamāyuktaḥ pacāmyannañcaturvidham II

> I am in all beings in the form of the digestive fire. Keeping the inhalation and exhalation in balance, I digest the food eaten in a fourfold way. II BG 15.14 II

This signifies that *Īśvara* is the digestive fire, ensuring that all beings are nourished and sustained. This is why we should not consume what is commonly referred to as "junk food." How can something be both junk and food at the same time? Our bodies are not garbage cans, therefore eating should be done with great mindfulness and quietude, treating it as a sacred act that honors *Īśvara*.

As a child I was raised to eat quietly and not talk while eating. But here, in the USA, people love to talk when they eat. When I first came to to this country, people often would say, "Let us talk about it over lunch." Initially, my first few lunch meetings did not go well because I was not accustomed to talking while eating. I was trained to remain silent during meals. Generally, you do not multitask or converse while eating.

Eating is worship. Cooking is worship. Taking care of children is worship. Work is worship. When you approach these activities with a sense of reverence and devotion, they become a form of yoga that destroys sorrow. This is stated in the Bhagavad-Gita: *yogo bhavati duḥkhahā*. *Karmayoga* is described as the destroyer of sorrow.

Question: What would be the way to remain cheerful 24/7, 365 days?

Answer: You do not have to worry about 24/7 because let us say you need 10 hours of sleep. Even if you sleep for eight hours, you need some time to wind down and calm yourself before that. So, you give yourself 10 hours, leaving 14 hours of active time.

Now, if you wake up in the morning and tell yourself, "I am going to be constantly cheerful for the next 14 hours," I guarantee that you will immediately feel like crawling back under the covers! This is because 14 hours of enforced cheerfulness is too much!

If one gives oneself a directive to remain cheerful for the next 14 hours, one will not even feel like getting out of bed. One would think, "What is the point? I cannot do this; it is overwhelming, it is too much." The mind is like a child. If a mother were to tell her toddler, "Honey, entertain yourself. Play with your toys. I will be back in 14 hours," the child would not even comprehend that. The mind also is like that.

What is the alternative? It is to cultivate the practice of being present now itself. I do not worry about the whole day. I am here now. We have already discussed some ways of being the present, but this point cannot be emphasized enough. Taking the time to breathe, watching the breath, watching the mind, being in nature, appreciating things in one's life, and doing *sevā* are all ways to bring the mind back to the present. Very soon, you find that 14 hours have gone by without even knowing it.

If one has some physical or emotional discomfort, it is good to localize it. The general tendency is to globalize the pain, to dramatize the emotions, and make a huge deal of it. With the committed study of Vedanta, all big deals become small deals.

Somebody asked me, "If I study Vedanta, will my problems go away?" I said, "No." "Oh!

Then why am I studying Vedanta?" "To discover that you are much bigger than your problems." If you are bigger than your problems, the problems become tiny, small, and insignificant. This is how we cultivate an attitude of cheerfulness by focusing on the present moment– on small things in the now, and by connecting to the largesse within.

Right now, am I hungry? No? That is good! Wonderful! If I catch myself wondering what I will eat tomorrow, I remind myself not to worry. Right now, I am not hungry, and the tummy is full. Now, there is no reason for agitation, scarcity, or worry. It is the scarcity mentality that eclipses cheerfulness. You are already cheerful; you just have to own it.

Question: I do not feel fear, and I do not feel sorrow. So, why do I need to connect with God?

Answer: It is commendable that you decided not to feel fear and sorrow. We have to make sure that we are not suppressing the feelings. It is one thing to say, "I am not going to give in to fear or sorrow. I am not going to be held hostage by sorrow. I am not going to be made a prisoner of this fear." If that is what you have decided, it is a wonderful goal. If that is not what you have decided, then we have to talk about it some more.

The *saṅkalpa– intention–* "I am not going to be under the grip of fear, I am not going to let sorrow have the last laugh and hold me as a prisoner," is a better than to say, "I am not going to feel fear or sorrow." If we were in charge of our feelings, then we would not need Vedanta at all. Everyone could simply make a *saṅkalpa* saying, "I am not going to feel fear. Bye bye sorrow! Farewell, anger!" Then who would need Vedanta? All the swamis would be out of a job.

We welcome all emotions. The emotions are a manifestation of *Bhagavān*. *Bhagavān* has given us emotions because they act like the safety valve of a pressure cooker. Without them, the pressure builds up and eventually blows the lid. Indian pressure cookers are known for this. When I was young, I remember being in the kitchen of a distressed neighbor. The whole kitchen was covered in yellow lentils. Mung dal had become the new kitchen wallpaper, and stuck to the ceiling was the lid of the pressure cooker.

This is what happens inside the person when there is no safe outlet for the feelings. It is not wrong to feel sad or afraid. You can feel these emotions as long as you do not hurt yourself or others. Inserting a few things there makes it a wonderful *saṅkalpa*, an intention, a *sādhana*, a practice.

Remember, you are never truly sad; you are *saccidānanda*. You are never truly afraid; you are *saccidānanda*. From the perspective of *saccidānanda* and the self, look at this little suffering being and say, "You'll be okay." You have to re-parent that part of you affected by sorrow or fear.

Question: **Swaminiji, how do we prevent ourselves from being affected by the world, especially by harsh words, which feel like they are consuming you?**

Answer: First, we need to shift our perspective– turn the premise on its head, like doing a headstand, *śīrṣāsana*. From now on, let us view the world as a manifestation of

Īśvara. There is no assault; it is not attacking us. Instead, it represents objectivity, not subjectivity, because it is the truth. The world is *Īśvara*.

The world operates through a series of orders. These orders are so vast and inclusive that they even encompass what we perceive as disorder.

When we see disorder as part of *Īśvara*'s order, we view things differently. For instance, if someone makes a painful comment, it feels like an attack. But in recognizing it as a part of the greater order, we can perceive it more objectively. If we label it as pure disorder, we react by thinking, "That was unfair. How dare you do this? How dare you say this?"

Understanding that even the unpleasant is within
the cosmic order helps us accept and deal with people and situations more effectively.

If we understand that the world's order occasionally includes a few "weirdos," some "crazies," and people who act in hurtful ways, we can adjust our expectations accordingly.

This transformation in expectation changes our perspective.

Recognizing that there will always be people, events, situations and objects that are inimical to us this does not make the world a bad or painful place to live. Instead, it helps us see that these challenging aspects are also part of the world's order.

By adjusting our expectations in light of the knowledge that the world is a manifestation of *Īśvara*, we can accept that even disorder is part of the cosmic order.

When you have this knowledge, if someone says something hurtful, you only need "local anesthesia," not "general anesthesia" to get over it. Think of it like applying a pain balm to a sore spot. You might acknowledge, "I know they should not have said that" and then give yourself a comforting hug. Maybe you can even make a few funny faces at them when you are by yourself. It might feel cathartic and help lighten the moment. Treating it this way makes the hurt a "local affair." You address the immediate pain and then move on, without letting it affect your overall well-being.

If you want to progress spiritually, you can go a little deeper. After the hurt has subsided, and you have comforted yourself, ask: "Why did this pain arise? Where did it come from?" Do not accept the first answer, which might be, "It came from that idiot over there." That is not the correct answer.

The root cause often lies in a deeper place– it could perhaps be a memory from childhood trauma, or it could be karmic, stemming from past actions. By reflecting in this way, you can understand and integrate this aspect of the pain, moving beyond surface reactions.

You hold this understanding for yourself and gradually allow the perception that the world is out to get you to drop. This approach leads to a much more balanced and sane way of living.

Everything changes, and you find a spring in your step and a smile on your face for no apparent reason. It is simple, really– just small shifts in perspective.

Question: My question is about smiling. It is sometimes very hard to keep smiling. My friend just messaged me, "I just lost my optic glasses in the water, but I am still smiling," she says. So, even when you have lost something and maybe you are sad, you put on a smile. Even if it is the hardest thing to do, it might not be a real smile, but you are forcing it.

Answer: Yes, I am glad you asked this question because there are two facets to this. My teacher always used to say, "Fake it till you make it." This means you do not feel like smiling but smile anyway because that is actually *ānanda*. You are already *ānanda*, and you are not really faking it. You think you are faking it, so smile anyway.

This is the general rule, but there are exceptions. If one comes from a family where smiling is a habitual pattern of denial– "Nothing to see here, nothing wrong, everything and everybody is fine, better smile, you too, you too, everybody should keep smiling"– then for a while, it is good not to smile.

If one has been brought up in a familial culture of denial, covered up by compulsive smiling, it is better to go against this habit by schooling the facial features to look like a rock on the side of the road. At least in the beginning, this might help one to get out of the habit of portraying a compulsive and ersatz happiness. It is not real happiness– it is a denial of difficulties.

For such people, I would say, for a while, do not smile. It is good to remember this. Eventually, you will start smiling again, but it will be a different smile– a deeper and more authentic smile. You will be smiling on your own terms because you want to, not because you have to.

Insult and Injury

Question: I have a question about what the Bhagavad-Gita says: the highest state of a *yogin* is bearing insult and injury. I do not quite understand how that applies in practical life.

Answer: In the 12th chapter, Lord Krishna says a *yogin* is one who is not affected by insult, or by injury:

> **तुल्यनिन्दास्तुतिर्मौनी सन्तुष्टो येन केनचित्।**
> **अनिकेतः स्थिरमतिः भक्तिमान् मे प्रियः नरः॥**
> *tulya-nindā-stutirmaunī santuṣṭo yena kenacit*
> *Ianiketaḥ sthira-matir bhaktimān me priyo*
> *naraḥ* II
>
> The person who is equanimous in censure and praise, disciplined in speech, satisfied with whatever there is, one who has no place to call as one's own, whose knowledge is firm and one who is full of devotion is beloved to me. II BG 12.19 II

A *yogin* is not one who looks for insults saying, "I am your doormat. Come and insult me." That is not a *yogin*; it is someone who needs a therapist. A *yogin* is mature and compassionate. If someone criticizes them, they do not take it personally, they do not suffer as a result. They do not think, "Oh no, why did they do this? Who are they to tell me off like this?" They do not hold grudges or get upset. Similarly, if someone praises them, they do not become overly elated.

Usually one is fishing for validation, one is a compliment-hunter. When someone praises the carpet, the homeowner gets happy. This shows how easily people can get elated. A *yogin* remains steady, unswayed by praise or criticism.

The *yogin* and the *jñānin*, the person of knowledge, have enough emotional maturity. Because of their *sarvātmabhāva*, there is inner security. Therefore, they do not get affected by criticism or praise. They remain the same, and cultivating this sameness is the key for one who wishes to be a *yogin*.

Fear and Anxiety

Question: I have a specific question. Let us say one is exposed to trauma– mental or physical– and is aware that this trauma manifests as fear and anxiety in certain situations. Just recognizing it is not enough, because the cycles keep repeating. How does one get free from these cycles?

Answer: The experience of trauma keeps one l ocked in cycles. We have to address it on different levels.

The body holds trauma at many levels. There is something known as cellular memory. Sometimes amputees experience this kind of pain, long after the limb is gone. It is a kind of a phantom pain that haunts in the form of memory. The practice of yoga teaches self-love, and *prāṇāyāma* is a great blessing that cultivates self-love and self-confidence to heal the trauma at the physical level.

Psychotherapy and journaling are *sādhana* for the mind, aiding in overcoming PTSD by preventing one from repeatedly reliving the trauma. Talking or writing a little bit every day is beneficial. When one is ready, pursuing these teachings and committing to Vedanta, surrendering to Vedanta eventually takes away trauma for good.

Over time, when you understand that this trauma is not you but something that happened to you, you can practice being a loving witness instead of being caught in non-acceptance. This is the first step. You will come to terms with the situation. Accepting what happened does not mean you did something wrong. No one deserves to be traumatized. It happened because of someone else's abuse of their free will, which you had to endure. Coming to terms with one's parentage and its meaning involves seeing it not just as a "present" from *Īśvara* but as the "presence" of *Īśvara*. That is what it is. *Īśvara* is your background today.

We have a prayer that says, *mātṛdevo bhava,* may you be the one for whom the mother is a manifestation of *Bhagavān; pitṛdevo bhava,* may you be the one for whom the father is a manifestation of *Bhagavān*. This reflects a profound inner maturity. It is truly amazing. What does it mean? It means that the person sees the mother as a manifestation of God, indicating they have come to terms with and accepted the mother exactly as she is or was. The same applies to the father. They accept the mother and father for who they are/were in their perception. In this acceptance, they give them the freedom to be who they are or who they were. By looking at it this way, they can look at the trauma objectively.

The parents who hurt you also had a background. If we visualize the father when he was five years old we can see this clearly. We may not even know what the father was like at age five, but we do know that, no matter his excesses, he too was an innocent and vulnerable child once. We can look upon this little boy with love, separating the person from the conduct, and in so doing the feelings of hurt have the potential to be transformed.

One can do the same thing for oneself. One can visualize oneself as a five year old child, and send it love and acceptance. This is an important part of inner-child work, which involves re-parenting the child within by gaining its trust. All this is necessary to be free of trauma, and to assimilate Vedanta.

Question: Can you get rid of trauma in one lifetime?

Answer: Yes, can happen, *tathāstu*!

Question: I was recently reminded that as human beings, we experience some type of concern or anxiety daily. I woke up smiling and feeling good. It was a concern from years ago that I thought was resolved, but it suddenly popped into my head. I was surprised. Why does that happen? When one concern seems to be solved, something you were not even aware of comes in to take your mind elsewhere.

Answer: Congratulations! I am glad it is resolved. I pray that this period of tranquility continues for you. Regarding your concern, why is it that we always have to be anxious about something? This is the first part of your question. The second part is why something from a long time ago can suddenly surface and surprise you, arriving without notice.

Why the memory came is not important. Treat the anxiety like you would treat an old school friend– someone you have not seen in a long time. Where was it all this time? It was latent, deeply buried in the unconscious mind, and then it got exhumed. Why did it get exhumed? Because there was a trigger. We may not know what the trigger is. In fact, trying to find out the trigger itself can be triggering, so I do not suggest that. If you are blessed to know the trigger, that is good. Even if you do not know the trigger, you are still blessed. There is some trigger, and the trigger is always in the present, which hooks into remnants from the past, bringing out that memory and anxiety.

Even though we think anxiety is a very big problem– making us lose sleep and peace of mind– we should see it as a gift. One more difficulty is on its way out. One more thing I do not have to worry about. One less thing to think about. This is how to approach it. It looks like you have done the right thing. Remember, anxiety is just another name for fear.

When fear is sensed, there are actually two things one is afraid of. One is afraid of the object of fear, and one is afraid of fear itself. Pujya Swamiji would tell you to welcome the fear. Make two cups of chai, one for you and one for the fear, and say, "Okay, it is tea time." I have had people do this, and it is very effective. I recommended this to a man in California, and he did it in a cafe. He went to a cafe, sat down, and ordered two coffees. Everyone thought a friend was coming. He had a wonderful session. He wrote down his thoughts and softly dictated them into his device. Everyone thought he was in an important meeting, and indeed it was a very important meeting. This approach works because you personify the fear, preventing anxiety from gripping the heart and throat. Most of the time, people are afraid of fear itself. To welcome fear, just say, "I am okay. What can you do to me? Come, let us be friends. Tell me what you are trying to tell me. What are you afraid of?"

This is how one can work with anxiety. The fear of fear causes a kind of paralysis. When that fear is removed, the issue at hand becomes manageable, like a pet dog. Then you find out what it needs: food, a walk, or something else. It simplifies the problem. This is how we work with anxiety.

Question: Swaminiji, you touched upon two things. One was the fear of the unknown, and the other was the urge to control whatever we can within our capacity. Whenever there is anxiety about the unknown, it turns into panic for me because I start overthinking all possible outcomes. Sometimes, this overthinking is worse than the actual fear of

the unknown itself. I understand that constant exposure to these teachings can help correct habitual errors.

Answer: I agree with you. Yes, and you are already doing the right thing, so there is no problem. You are listening to everything you can possibly listen to. The analytical mind is both a blessing and a challenge. It is a blessing because it helps one to appreciate these teachings and assimilate them. It is a challenge because it is a noose around the same neck that wants to be free of it.

The next time you feel the need to control, invite that fear. Have a cup of chai with it. That is the first suggestion. The second thing one can do is to convert the time spent on analysis into *japa*. Watch your mind and say, "I am worried about this," and then attach "*Oṁ namaḥ śivāya*" at the end. Say, "I am worried about this, I am really obsessing about this, '*Oṁ namaḥ śivāya*.' I let it go," even if it comes back. Keep saying, "I am still worried about this. This is not going away, '*Oṁ namaḥ śivāya*.' I am letting it go." Do this as many times as it takes.

Convert your thoughts into *Īśvara*. *Īśvarize* the mind. See the mind and all its thoughts as manifestations of *Īśvara*. Surrender the mind to *Īśvara* and say, "O *Īśvara*, O Lord, O Goddess, you who have given me this mind, please take care of it. Make it turn firmly to all that which is auspicious. Make my mind in tandem with your will. Fix my mind to seek the most auspicious *mokṣa*."

Chapter 12
VEDANTA IN EVERYDAY LIFE

Discernment

Question: How to know when to intervene and when it is not my job to interfere in any given situation?

Answer: Life does not come with an instruction booklet. We have some general guidance in what is called *sāmānya-dharma*, the universal matrix of norms that guides us about what is right and wrong. In Western countries, this is understood as the golden rule: do unto others what you want them to do unto you; do not do unto others what you do not want to be done to you. Since dharma is not static, *sāmānya-dharma* needs to be interpreted properly and applied to different situations. This is called *viśeṣa-dharma*. Often, one is confused about how to apply universal dharma to specific situations. We learn by watching *vṛddha-vyavahāra*, the conduct of elders who are role models in the family and the society. Since ours is a culture that has a high regard for dharma, we tend to be on the cautious side so as not to make errors by intervening in inappropriate situations.

The general rule of thumb for a *jijñāsu,* a seeker of knowledge, is to mind one's own business. We can focus on numerous things in our own life that require intervention–habits that no longer serve us in our quest for knowledge can be dropped, *śraddhā,* trust in the words of the teacher and the teaching can be cultivated. We can also focus on training the mind to be tranquil and receptive, making it easy to assimilate the teachings. Minding one's own business is a beautiful *tapas,* a discipline that has many benefits. First, it helps reduce the stronghold of *rāga-dveṣa* in the *antaḥkaraṇa*, starting with the desire to embroil oneself in various situations that are irrelevant to one's life and one's goals. Next, minding one's own business has the potential to cultivate *samādhana,* focus. Finally, it also helps in emotional growth by taming the validation-seeking *ahaṅkāra,* which seeks to control situations and get enmeshed in them. There are some exceptions where one can consider intervention. Obviously, if one is in the role of a parent or teacher, one has to intervene to instruct people in one's charge.

Another exception, where one can consider intervening is if it is a dangerous situation, in which you are able to help. For example, if a child or an elder has fallen and there is no one around, you can intervene. Situations such as someone being in danger, a child crossing the road alone, or an animal being hurt or trapped require immediate attention. In such cases, I would err on the side of intervening, rather than waiting and watching. In other situations, one can wait and see.

If someone is in danger and you are in a safe place with the power to help, you can intervene. However, if it is a dangerous situation and you are not equipped to protect yourself, or you do not know what to do, you can call emergency services, such as the police or the ambulance. This is also a productive and pragmatic intervention.

Question: In the society, if you are playing a role and are empowered to do that role, is it okay to intervene even if you know it may go wrong, and you may be attacked?

Answer: There are many ways of intervening. The nicest way is to do it in a very polite manner, without making a splash. First, try that approach. But if you are in a position of leadership, expect to be attacked. If you are in a leadership position and you are not attacked, consider it a rare stroke of luck. Usually, if one is in a leadership position, there will be some projections.

Bhagavān has put you in a position of leadership because you are strong enough to handle attacks and not take them personally. When a leader is attacked, we have to understand that the attack stems from the other person's background.

You do not have to know what their background is. They have a background, which is why they behave like this. This much knowledge is enough. With this objectivity, you do not take attacks personally. The whole purpose of Vedanta in action is to depersonalize things in every situation, in every relationship by understanding that one is not being targeted.

In time we appreciate the fact that the other person is going through something, which is the cause of what they said or did. We can be the bigger person and overlook it. We can grow to let it go.

Question: Do you have any advice for someone who struggles with decision-making?

Answer: Indecision often stems from insecurity. There can be many reasons for indecision, but the most common one is insecurity. People think that no matter what they decide, they are making a mistake. Along with insecurity, there is often perfectionism. Everyone wants to get things right and perfect immediately. That is why Mark Twain said, "Please make a new mistake every day." Make as many mistakes as you want but do not repeat the same mistakes; make new ones. Indecision arising from insecurity is often tied to perfectionism and a fear of making mistakes.

Another cause of indecision is a lack of trust. It is a trust issue. People do not trust their own judgment. These causes are interrelated. I am just highlighting some of them. A person might not trust their own judgment, and even if someone else offers advice, they still do not trust it. They ask, "What do you think I should do?" and even when they get an answer, they are unable to discern whether the advice is sound for them. Sometimes, the issue is not really about not knowing what to do– it is about trust.

Another reason for indecision is the fear of committing to one particular solution, one way of life, or one person. This fear is especially rampant in contemporary times. People do not want to commit; they want to be free-floating entities, like a rolling stone that gathers no moss. They do not want to be bound to something they might later regret. This fear of commitment often loops back to the fear of making the wrong choice or a mistake. You can see how complex this whole issue of indecision is? It is complex enough to give one complexes.

The fear of missing out on something better is yet another reason for chronic indecision. In America it is called FOMO. People think, "If I do this, then that means I cannot do that, because both choices are either opposed one another or are happening at the same time." This constant state of being on the fence leads one to being defensive. What we do not understand properly is that when there is difficulty making decisions, taking the stance "I am not going to decide" is also a decision. Choosing not to decide is a decision to let circumstances dictate the direction of your life. It is a decision to be apathetic and to not participate actively in your own life. This default decision arises from being confronted with multiple choices or being unable to choose between two options, leading to paralysis and inaction.

What fun is there in this apathy? It is dangerous because opportunities pass by, and one misses them. This can spiral into emotional pain, depression and feeling victimized. The apathy leads to a downward spiral where one is not pursuing goals, ambitions, or dreams, resulting in sadness.

Therefore, when faced with indecision, extra prayers are needed.

What if one is making the wrong choice? It does not matter. If you make the wrong choice, pray, and accept that you lacked sufficient information or *viveka*, discernment. No one intentionally makes wrong decisions. If you do not have enough information, wait, but not indefinitely. Waiting for three lifetimes to decide is not the idea. Wait until you gain some clarity. But if clarity never comes because you are stuck in patterns, take a leap of faith. Pray and take action, using practices we follow in India.

We have a kind of *Bhagavān/Īśvara* oracle. A word of caution: the oracle is not to be used for mundane issues like deciding whether to have Italian or Mexican food for dinner. If you cannot decide that, even *Bhagavān* will not be able to help. This is a method for difficult decisions.

If you face a choice between two options, take two identical pieces of paper and write binary answers: "yes" on one piece of paper, and "no" on the other. Write a keyword of the first choice on one paper and a keyword of the second choice on another. Do not cheat. Fold them identically, mix them up, say a prayer, put them in front of the altar, close your eyes, and pick one. Follow what it says. One needs to trust something, to prevent constant indecision from taking over one's life.

We need to take matters into our own hands, and if we lack confidence, leave it to *Bhagavān*. Use the two pieces of paper method. If you feel that the wrong choice has come up, and you think, "I will take the best of three," and you repeat it three times, and still, the less favorite choice comes up, you might say, "Okay, best of five." If the same choice keeps coming up, it means you already know what you want to do. This is great. Congratulations! Either way, the method works. Either it will help you decide, or it will reveal what you really wanted but were afraid to embrace. Surrender it to *Bhagavān* and trust that it will not go wrong. Even if it does go wrong, it is not wrong. It is *sthāne*, it is in place to learn the lesson one needs at that time.

Question: Swaminiji, my mother is a student of yours. I had to take a medical retirement. Since my time off, I have become much more committed to a spiritual life, and I feel like that is a good path for me. However, in my husband's family, nobody even knows how to spell the word Vedanta. I feel like I am the only person in my world trying to purify my mind and life. I have stuck to the same mantra, and I keep doing the same thing every day, but I am still confused by the world around me. Regarding my personal choices, how do I know if it is my *ātman* guiding me, or if it is just my impure mind making these decisions for me?

Answer: You do not have an impure mind, first of all. It is very clear you have had wonderful *saṃskāras*, given by your parents. The mind can have some indecision, definitely, because as observed, you have no allies, no companions to share this path, and no satsang, being around like-minded people. Studying in a group is something very special. Zoom also helps a bit because you see little postage stamp-sized images of people's faces, and you realize that you are not isolated. That is why, even though there is Zoom, people still like to come and sit in the presence of the teacher. Perhaps that is missing for you, and that is why your mind is going here, there, and everywhere.

The best thing to do is to be a mother to that mind. Just like when a baby is tired and cranky, you lull it, pat it on the back, and put it to sleep. Similarly, allow the doubts in your mind to go to sleep. Use the *mantra* as a pacifier for the cranky mind. The mind is unstable, that is all. Sit with *japa*, establish a routine that is self-affirming. It is difficult when there is nobody else around you who practices Vedanta, but we are all here with you. I am with you, and if I can be of any service in any way, let me know. We have many classes here, and all the satsangs are broadcast. You can access everything, including the classes, on YouTube.

All you have to do is be gentle with yourself and put yourself on a diet of Vedanta for breakfast, lunch, and dinner. Listen to one or two classes a day, follow a text, and you can be on the right path.

Communicating Effectively

Question: I have a practical question. This is my first time at an ashram and my first time listening to your teachings, which I found extraordinarily enlightening and mind-blowing. I have loved my time here. I was speaking to my husband last night, who is a very logical, scientific person. He asked me questions, and I told him I was enjoying myself so much that I am staying two more days. I am really excited about it, and he asked, "Oh, am I losing you?" There was fear in him that I was changing, but we had a wonderful conversation. It is all good, but I thought it was interesting. I was wondering if you could speak to how we can communicate clearly what we are learning here to those we love.

Answer: This is a very important question. Many people may be in that situation, even if they are not staying for two extra days. If one person is enjoying it more, how can they avoid making the significant other feel threatened? This is important. If one person is interested in a partnership and the other is growing out of it due to Vedanta, what should be done? My suggestion would be, while it is wonderful you stayed these two days, you should make up for it when you go back. Give a lot of time, attention and love, and express gratitude for your partner's broad mind and big heart that allowed you to do this. Without the partner's cooperation, you would not have been able to do this.

Tell your husband this teaching is about growing into a loving and compassionate being. Everyone can go and tell their spouses this, and then immediately, there will be a kind of nuclear disarmament. "Oh, it is about loving! Oh, it is about compassion!"

But you see, only talking about joy, love and compassion is not enough because the spouse and children have a different kind of radar. They do not respond to talk. You can talk till all the cows come home, but what is important is to walk the talk. It is not enough to say, "I am learning about compassion and love, and these are the hallmarks of self-knowledge and enlightenment," You have to demonstrate that in your interactions with them, and make them a partner in your self-growth.

For example, you might say, "I am trying very hard to live by the tenets of the Bhagavad-Gita, and when you see me slipping, please tell me." You give them the freedom to do that. If they say, "See, you are getting angry," you should respond with, "Yes, you are right."

Even if you feel like it, this is not the time to say, "Who asked you? You are also getting angry." It is the time to say, "Let us make a family pact: if I am getting angry and not noticing it, you please feel free to tell me, and I will do the same for you." In this way, a time will come when the children and spouse will say to you, "Please go to your ashram for a retreat; you are a little irritable and stressed." They begin to see that each time you go for a retreat, they also benefit from it. They will themselves send you, because they see the value in it.

Another thing we need to understand is to let the spouse win every argument from now onwards. It is worth it because it is a win-win situation. Why is it a win-win? Because your commitment now, after coming to a place like this and after listening to the teachings, is self-growth.

Your commitment is not to win an argument. So, if you let them win, saying, "Yes honey, you are right," they will think, "Oh, this ashram is really good," and they will be very benevolent towards your spiritual path. That is one big win. Another win is for you because you grow as a result of being disappointed that you did not get your way. It is a double-win situation.

Once, in Atlanta, I was talking about this and said, "Be the first one to lose an argument." There was a newly married couple in the audience, and both their hands shot up at once. I said, "Yes, what is your question?" They had the same question: "Who should lose the argument first?"

This is how you bring people along with you. You do not leave them behind. It is very easy to say, "I am having a special experience, and you are not," and then put people off. We do not need to do that. We bring people along slowly, gently, and lovingly. Next time, bring your family with you. Even if they go to the beach the whole day. It does not matter; they will be physically here with you and that matters.

Question: I am a mother of two kids, and each one thinks I love the other more. That is not the case. They are at an age where they are getting into college and being on their own. I do not want them to have that lingering feeling. What can I do to prevent this impression?

Answer: You are already doing whatever is needed. If you wear yourself out trying to please both of them, they may still feel that way. One of them might say, "When the other one came, you cooked this, but when I came, this was not done," or "Whenever I come, you are so busy, but when the sibling comes, you have all the time in the world." This feeling is going to be there, so what to do? One option is to not have children, then you do not have this worry. But this is not an option in this case.

When a situation of envy or jealousy arises, smile at both of them and say, "Your feeling of lack is very valid. Even Krishna and Balarama felt the same way." Take it back to history. Rama and his siblings also felt the same way. Normalize the feeling and say it is normal and part of their own karmic journey to sort out. If you remain uninvolved in their conflict, they might look at each other and think maybe you do not favor either of them. As a result, they may bond, which is exactly what you want.

We grow emotionally to drop the desperate desire to be loved and validated by the children. Instead, we validate them because that is what they need as they are growing.

Question: I want to know how to deal with people who repeatedly seek your advice, and when you give it to them, they do not take it. If it is a family member, and you cannot avoid interacting with such a person, what to do in that situation?

Answer: Admittedly, this is difficult because they come to you and ask for advice. You, being the good samaritan, give the advice, but then they do not take it and ask again.

Think of them as being placed there by *Bhagavān* to enhance your spiritual growth by leaps and bounds. Thank them. Give them flowers next time and say, "Thank you for contributing to my *titikṣā*." *Titikṣā* is having the patience of a saint. Thank them for helping you cultivate *titikṣā* by force, because nobody would choose to develop patience voluntarily. Pujya Swamiji would say that even if someone prayed for patience, the prayer might sound like, "O God! Give me patience, I want it Right Now!"

We can thank people in our lives who we cannot avoid, because their presence has the potential to accelerate spiritual growth in a way that even *Bhagavatī* could not. That is why she has placed them there, so you will grow. Over time, you will learn to respond patiently without censure, annoyance, or worry. Each time, we learn to speak to them as if it is the first time they are approaching for advice. Treat each conversation as a fresh one. When you do this, you start responding rather than reacting to the situation.

Obviously, the advice given one time was not enough, and the second time was not either.

Your whole life, you may keep telling them the same thing, but it may never be enough. You will become a very patient person. As you gain that patience, you can recognize that seeking advice may be a pattern for the person. They keep coming to you but do not heed the advice you give. We can ask ourselves whether our advice is helping, or whether we are in fact contributing to their problem.

When you are healed enough not to fall into this pattern of automatically, you can respond differently. Next time they come to you and say, "I am desperate, everything is going wrong, help!" you can say, "What do you think? How would you approach this? You are so bright and intelligent! In fact, I know you are brilliant. The answers are within you, and I am here to listen."

Let them talk, and you listen. Perhaps that will break the pattern.

World Disorder

Question: Thank you again for your time being here. My question relates to the state of today's world. When we look at humanity, it seems like humanity has never seen so much change in such a short period of time. At the same time, the world is so polarized. You can look at the political sphere, and wherever you look globally, there are extremes of the super-rich and the super-poor. There are incredible challenges that the world faces, like climate change and sustainable development goals. What is at the source of these issues? There are a lot of symptoms, but what is at the source, and what is something that can actually move the needle?

Answer: In every generation, we think, "Oh! This is the worst crisis that can ever happen." If there are some nonagenarians sitting and talking over chai, they will also think, "Oh! That was the worst time we went through." So, I think that it is a cycle. It keeps happening.

This whole global warming issue also happened earlier. They say fossils show that the Arctic was once green, not what we see now. Each time a glacier breaks down, our hearts break because we know we are dependent on a certain climate pattern that sustains us. This is part of what we call the *jagat– jāyate, gacchati iti jagat.* The *jagat* is that which is born, and then gone. It will always be changing. It changes for better or worse, depending on our perspective.

We may say all this is terrible, but someone else might think, "It is not too bad for me. I am fine." Financially they might be in the top one percent and feel unaffected. So, as long as we are in this *jagat*, these cycles will continue. This is what is called *kāla-cakra*, the wheel of time.

The *jagat* itself has collective karma, of which we are a part. Polarized partisanship is part of this karma, and now we are experiencing the Coronavirus karma. Who knew before 2019 that there would be such a thing called Coronavirus? We had no idea that we would not be able to be with each other and that we would have to stay in our homes. If anyone had said that, we would have laughed in their faces. But it is a collective, global karma– not a single country, group, or island has been left out. This is collective karma.

Just like this, there will be collective karmas intersecting with individual karmas. Change itself is the essence of what is called *jagat*. The crucial point, as you mentioned, is to understand what will move the needle in this scenario. The answer is to know that one is changeless. We respond to change by anchoring ourselves in the knowledge that the self is not subject to change. This is the gift of Vedanta. Equipped with this gift, we can remain centered and unaffected by the changes around us.

Having said that, there are individual responsibilities that come with being a world citizen, a citizen of a particular country, a member of a state, a community, and a family. We have responsibilities. We cannot just say, "Oh, the climate is changing and nothing will happen if I recycle one plastic bottle." If everyone thought like this, then definitely nothing would happen. It takes a lot of sacrifice and a commitment to change. We need to be open to the challenges of the time and see what we can do.

What am I capable of doing? What is my duty? What must I do? What can I do? What do I want to do? We always respect people who take action, like the environmentalist, Greta Thunberg. When she started her activism, she was only 14 years old. She is full of enthusiasm and hope.

Vedanta does not tell us to stay aloof; it says to participate in everything, but to let go of the expectation that things will turn out a certain way. Adjusting our expectations in the light of the outcome is the definition of sanity. When expectations are adjusted, there is no disappointment. It gives the impetus to continue doing what one is doing while still expecting an outcome. If that outcome falls short, we just try again or try a different approach.

Knowing the vision of Vedanta, that I am limitless and absolute, is crucial. Everything that is changing will continue to change. A healthy perspective is about the balance between taking something seriously and not taking it too seriously, cultivating a lucid sense of humor.

Chapter 13
BHAGAVĀN, BRAHMAN, ĪŚVARA

Are Brahman and Īśvara Synonyms?

Question: What is the difference between Brahman and *Bhagavān*? To be free of *saṃsāra*, do I need to know myself as Brahman or as *Īśvara*?

Answer: The word Brahman refers to consciousness that is free of attributes. Its *svarūpa,* intrinsic nature, is *satyam, jñānam anantam*, a sentient and limitless existence, whose implied meaning is the word "I." Seen from the standpoint of the universe, however, Brahman gains an incidental definition as *jagatkāraṇa*, the cause of the universe, which is incidental, which comes and goes. The first definition is known as *svarūpalakṣaṇa*, and the second one is called *taṭasthalakṣaṇa.*

As the cause of the universe, Brahman as-though gains attributes such as causality, omniscience, power, etc., which are called *bhaga*. The one endowed with bhaga in full measure is *Bhagavān*. The *bhagas are mithyā*. They contribute to *Īśvaratva,* the status of being *Īśvara*. We have to bear in mind that *Īśvaratva* is also *mithyā,* an apparent reality that is not independent of consciousness, which is free of all attributes. Therefore there is no mix-up because Brahman as-though appears as *Bhagavān* only with reference to the manifest universe, without itself undergoing any change. Brahman does not "become" *Bhagavān.*

The Upanishads equate *jīva* with *Īśvara*. The *jīva,* the individual, feels alienated and disconnected, and therefore the teaching seeks to show that the truth of the *jīva* and the truth of *Īśvara* are one and the same. Pujya Swamiji used to illustrate this point with the analogy of the wave and the ocean. Seen from the standpoint of the wave, it is one of many; if it had a human mind, it would compare itself to other waves, and have an inferiority complex. It would look at the ocean and feel small and finite. Suppose this wave were taught that it is none other than the ocean, at first it would be incredulous and would think thus: "How can I, a small wave, be the limitless ocean?" When it would be taught that the truth of the wave and the ocean is water, it would then understand itself as non-separate from the ocean. In the same way, if the *jīva* is told, "you are the formless Brahman," it is only a partial teaching. In order to be totally free of sorrow, the *jīva* has to comprehend that the truth of *Īśvara* is also the formless Brahman. Then only the teaching is complete.

Īśvara is essentially free of name and form, and therefore can be invoked through any name, or form. On the individual side also, we have to understand that Brahman, formless consciousness, is expressing itself through this particular name and this particular form at a given time. The name and form are *mithyā*. The name and form have to be transcended to understand the oneness.

Question: What are *Bhagavān*, Brahman, and *Īśvara?*

Answer: They are all synonymous. There is really no difference. *Bhagavān* means the one who has *bhaga*. *Bhaga* means auspiciousness or virtues such as omniscience, omnipotence, omnipresence in complete measure. The one who is limitlessly knowledgeable, limitlessly whole, has limitless resources, limitless *vairāgya*, limitless strength, etc., is *Bhagavān*. There are six *bhagas* that are talked about and the wielder of them is *Bhagavān*. He is the one who created this universe. The term refers to the active caretaker, creator, and resolver of the universe. This is *Bhagavān*.

Then we have the word *Īśvara*. "*Īś*" is a root verb which means the one who is overlord, the one who has all glories. *Vara* means always. *Īś* means the one who nurtures and nourishes. So, *Īśvara* is the one who is always nourishing the whole universe.

These two epithets are for the creator. They are related to the universe where there is an active connection between the creator and the created.

The final term is Brahman. Brahman means that which is limitlessly big. It can refer to both *Īśvara*– the creator, sustainer, and resolver– and to consciousness. free of all attributes underlying both the *jīva*, the crazy, complaining person, and *Īśvara*, the sane one without complaints. That same consciousness – untethered by complexes, sorrow, and fear – is Brahman.

When we say Brahman, it can refer to *Īśvara* in a manifest form or *Īśvara* in a latent form between cycles of creation. But really when we say Brahman, it refers to the only reality that is.

Ātman is a synonym for Brahman, from the standpoint of a individual body-mind-sense complex. Therefore, *ātman* is Brahman, and this is the teaching of Vedanta. Brahman is *Bhagavān*, without the accoutrements of overlordship and the power to create. But really, Brahman is *Īśvara*, and can be used for both the manifest *Īśvara* and the latent *Īśvara* as well.

Chapter 14
BHAKTI AND JÑĀNA

Is Bhakti a Path to Mokṣa?

Question: I have a question about the paths of *bhakti* and *jñāna*. We come across examples like Mirabai, Kabir, Rumi, Tukaram, and Chaitanya Mahaprabhu, who followed the path of *bhakti* and became enlightened. How can we do that? Is *bhakti* alone enough for a modern human being? Let us say a person follows both *jñāna* and *bhakti,* can we combine them for gaining knowledge?

Answer: We have to understand that the fundamental human problem is self-ignorance– not knowing that one is really not bound; one is already free. The seeker and the sought being the same, other than removing self-ignorance, there are no options for self-knowledge. *Karmayoga, bhakti, dhyāna,* etc. are auxiliary means for cultivating the temperament and preparedness needed to receive the knowledge. *Bhakti,* devotion, is a crucial step for gaining *jñāna,* but that is not to say that the two combine to remove self-ignorance. We have to be very clear that self-ignorance is removed by self-knowledge.

Suppose I have a pair of glasses perched on my head, and having forgotten all about them, I keep looking for them everywhere. Searching for the glasses is not going to produce the glasses. No amount of *prayer, tapas* or singing *bhajans* will bring back the glasses. The only thing that will "produce" the glasses is someone telling me that they are already perched on my head. The glasses are as-though lost and are as-though found. It is the same situation with self-ignorance. The self-evident self is already free, yet I do not know this and suffer from a sense of bondage, and therefore have to be told about the nature of myself by a guru.

Further, there is no such thing as a *bhakti* path that is an exclusive pursuit. What would the *bhaktas,* the devotees, do? Let us say that they do *pūjā*. Ritualized worship is *kāyika-karma,* physical action. Perhaps the *bhakta* sings *bhajans*– that is also karma, *vācika-karma,* verbal action. Perhaps the *bhakta* sits and does *japa*. This would be *mānasa-karma,* mental action. Since the expression of *bhakti* is tethered to karma, we cannot characterize *bhakti* as a separate path.

We cannot also come to the conclusion that the saints you mention gained knowledge through *bhakti*. Saint Mirabai had a guru; she talks about studying with her guru. Saint Kabir had a guru, and Chaitanya Mahaprabhu also had a guru. It is incorrect to say that *bhakti* and *jñāna* are separate paths. In our minds, we have an artificial distinction between *bhakti* saints and *jñāna* saints. This is not the reality. The reality is that even though we call them *bhakti* saints, they never called themselves that. *Bhakti* is highlighted because they expressed their *jñāna,* they delighted in their knowledge through devotional songs and poetry.

Devotion becomes an indirect gateway for knowledge, which is wonderful, but that does not mean these saints did not have teachers or they did not study Vedanta. Everybody had a teacher, and they also talked about it; they sang about it.

Bhakti as a separate path was popularized by Swami Vivekananda as a strategic response to the times in which he lived. In those days there was a lot of spiritual laxity, *tamas*. We were being ruled by the British. People were going away from dharma, away from this knowledge. Swami Vivekananda wanted to inspire people and awaken them from their apathetic stupor. Therefore, he emphasized two other paths that are not really talked about by the Upanishads.

The Upanishads talk about two committed lifestyles for gaining this knowledge: one is to dive directly into the river of knowledge and let the Upanishad churn you, and turn you into a *śiva-liṅga*. Or you gain the knowledge while pursuing other goals.

How does one do this? Recall the airport story. On the way to the airport, you may do many things, but you always know the flight is at a certain time. No matter where you go or what all you do, you are still headed to the airport. Similarly, *mokṣa*– liberation from *saṃsāra*– is the goal at all times, through the fulfillment of various desires, such as education, job, marriage, or children.

For the ones unable to commit to *mokṣa* as full time pursuit, taking small steps towards self-knowledge is recommended. You may be unable to commit to it wholly, so you do it little by little. Bit by bit, while pursuing other desires and duties, you are a mother, a father, a spouse, an employer, or an employee. All these roles are there, but you still want to be liberated.

Therefore, you use all these instances in your life to grow. That is why I said that it is good to let the spouse win all the arguments in the house. It promises marital peace and self-growth at the same time because the point is not winning the argument; the point is self-growth. You use every opportunity and every interaction for self-growth. These are the only two paths, and this is iterated in the *Īśāvāsya* Upanishad:

> **कुर्वन्नेवेह कर्माणि जिजीविषेच्छतं समाः।**
> *kurvanneveha karmāṇi jijīviṣecchataṃ samāḥ* ।

By continuing to do karma may one live for a hundred years. II IU 2 II

This is *karmayoga*. By continually doing whatever I have to do, I grow. I live for a hundred years, and I keep growing into this destiny, which is *mokṣa*, freedom from *saṃsāra*.

तेन त्यक्तेन भुञ्जीथा मा गृधः कस्यस्विद्धनम्।
tena tyaktena bhuñjīthā mā gṛdhaḥ kasyasviddhanam **।**

May one protect the self by renunciation. `Do not covet the wealth of another.

II IU 1 II

I protect the self. This is very interesting. I protect the self by giving everything up. How do you protect the self by giving everything up? The more one hoards, the harder it is to be on this path of knowledge. It is a path of total and complete *vairāgya,* dispassion.

According to the *śāstra*, there are only these two paths. You can be on the *Mokṣa-Express*, a bullet-train, or you can be on the *mokṣa* milk-train, which will take a long time to reach its destination, as it stops at every single station. It is okay; the main thing to note is that the milk-train also reaches the same destination. The lifestyle one chooses depends on one's preparation and sense of urgency.

Bhakti is common to both paths. Without being a *bhakta*, you cannot be a *karma-yogin* or a *jñāna-yogin*. You just cannot. *Bhakti* is essential. The *Īśvarization* of the whole universe is absolutely needed, and *Īśvarization* cannot happen without devotion. How can I see everything as *Īśvara* if I do not have devotion? Devotion, therefore, must be cultivated regardless of whether one is choosing *karmayoga* as a path or going straight to knowledge full-time. Devotion prepares you for knowledge. No *mukti* without *bhakti;* no devotion, no knowledge.

Chapter 15
THE VISION OF VEDANTA

Assimilation of Self-Knowledge

Question: How do you get established in the knowledge?

Answer: It is through *śravaṇa,* which means listening to the teachings of the Upanishads from a qualified teacher. When in doubt, resort to *śravaṇa*. The next day, if you ask, what is for breakfast? It is *śravaṇa*. What is for lunch? *Śravaṇa*. What is for dinner? *Śravaṇa*.

This is not about reading. Nothing happens if you are just reading the Upanishad because one gets in one's own way. It is a waste of time. After all that reading, it will be business as usual! You have to listen to a person who is qualified to give you that knowledge. You have to listen– there is no way around it. Thanks to the pandemic, all the gurus are coming to your home on Zoom, and therefore, all you have to do is to choose a guru and keep listening.

Question: What about the other way around? We keep hearing the knowledge so many times, we get it sometimes, and then it is gone.

Answer: It is not gone. It is there. It may appear to be "as though" gone. When the sun is eclipsed twice a year, you do not say the sun has gone. Early humans might have thought that. Cave men and cave women were likely agitated during an eclipse because they did not know any better. However, humanity now understands that an eclipse comes and goes.

This knowledge is "as though" eclipsed by the force of our likes, dislikes, fears, sorrow, agenda, and the unconscious mind. We work on cleansing the inner infrastructure so that there is darshan– the sighting– of *Bhagavān* within the thick forest of strong preferences and prejudices. *Bhagavān* is already there; you just have to clear the way. It will happen. It is already happening.

Question: I am just wondering about pursuing this knowledge. On one hand, we hear that people on this path already have the requisite *saṃskāras*. Also, some say that the horoscope indicates you are supposed to pursue this path in this lifetime, while others say we should go beyond the horoscope. Please clarify Swaminiji.

Answer: The fact that you are here means you have the *saṃskāra* for self-knowledge, for *ātmajñāna*. It is simple. The horoscope is like a blueprint of what can be. That is all. Liberation from pain and sorrow, called *saṃsāra*, is desired. *Saṃsāra* means some sorrow or the other. Liberation from *saṃsāra* is a *puruṣārtha*, something voluntarily desired and pursued.

Seeking liberation is based on free will, not on the horoscope. It is not based on *prārabdha*– it is not that some people are destined to be liberated, while others are not. In this sense, *mokṣa* is not karmic. It is not a fruit of action; rather it is a fruit of self-knowledge. Karma can perhaps indicate that a person has a spiritual predilection, but we have to remember that the person has the free will to either fully pursue this path or not pursue it at all. The freedom is always there. As many choices are possible, the horoscope has no way of knowing what kind of choice the person will make.

It is like this with every *puruṣārtha*. Whether it is dharma, *artha*, or any *puruṣārtha*, by seeing the placement of Jupiter, the other planets, and aspects, we can say the person has a dharmic predisposition. Still, other influences, such as socialization, can lead the person astray. For example, a person may have a dharmic bent of mind, but if the baby is born into a family of pickpockets, what will happen? First, a person is raised to be a pickpocket, and then they can eventually drop the habit because *puṇya* for the dharmic temperament kicks in.

These are all latent possibilities indicated by the horoscope. You cannot tell from the horoscope that a particular person is going to achieve *mokṣa*. You cannot tell that because this pursuit is based on free will. *Mokṣa* is a *puruṣārtha*, not based on *prārabdha*. It is not something destined; it is something you desire. You use your free will and decision-making process to pursue it.

Question: How does one repose in self?

Answer: It is very easy to repose in the self. In fact, you are reposing in the self as we speak. The self being all-pervasive, there is no way of not being with the self. On the contrary, the question should be, "How do I get out of myself?" Because wherever you are, whatever you do, the self is never away from you. In the Upanishad, there is a vākya: *sākṣād aparōkṣād brahma*, meaning what we call Brahman is right there. In *Dṛg-Dṛśya-Viveka*, there is a verse:

> **यत्र यत्र मनो याति तत्र तत्र समाधयः ॥**
>
> ***yatra yatra mano yāti tatra tatra samādhayaḥ*** **॥**
>
> Wherever the mind goes, there is *samādhi*.
>
> ॥ DDV 30 ॥

The difference between subject and object no longer exists; the object resolves into the subject, and all that remains is the subject. Then there is no subject because the word "subject" implies a relationship with an object.

Because of the contemporary lifestyle being with oneself is challenging. Even if you are sitting still, the mind is running. The phone has numerous messages, and the mind is going everywhere. Everyone thinks, "But if I do not check my messages now, later there will be a hundred messages." Let them be! "How can I allow there to be so many messages? When will I respond to all of them?" It is okay; it is not the end of the world. "If I do not respond, then people will stop texting me." Let them stop. The people sending the messages are also acting out of habit because they find that you are always available. It is not their fault; we have trained others to keep texting because we have been responding.

We must look at what is being filled when all these messages come. What void is being filled? Some Facebook updates come, filling a need. It is filling a void, alright, but at the cost of making me avoid the self. One becomes an avoidant personality because the messages prevent one from being connected to one's internal life.

One always wants to feel needed, and if this need is not interrogated, then being active on social media fills the purpose of feeling needed. "Oh! how nice! 50 people want me right now!" But it is "how nice" for whom? Not for the people, because one is encouraging codependency, and not for oneself, because one's *sādhana* is being disturbed. Therefore, we begin by letting go of extraneous things, by disengaging the emotional hold that one has on all activities, and letting meaningless pursuits drop.

As we grow up, we keep replacing one addiction with another, and often it comes to a standstill with the smartphone. The makers of these phones are very clever; that is why they put an "i" in front of it and call it iPhone. The iPhone is trying to replace I, *ātman*. We have iMac, iPod, iTunes, and iPad. Without the iPad, I am mad. We allow these companies and capitalism to exploit us emotionally.

The *Muṇḍakopaniṣad* instructs us by saying, *anyā vāco vimuñcatha,* give up all other talk. We might conclude that if we cannot talk, we can communicate through text. That is also not allowed. You give up all these extraneous things, and one way to do it is to decide only to talk about Vedanta.

Topics such as *ātman,* Brahman, Upanishad, or Gita, are often unpopular with the general public, and therefore, if you keep talking of Vedanta, friends and colleagues may think that you are a big bore. At first, even if you feel like this is not what you signed up for, that is exactly what you want. Otherwise, you would not be here or have an interest in studying Vedanta. This way, you do not have to break up with anybody. Slowly, addictions to people and things drop on their own. It is not that you are shunning your friends. You are talking about what is wonderful for you and wish to revel in the teachings. That is why you are talking about them.

You allow things to drop because if people do not wish to go on this journey with you, it is not worth leaving the study of Vedanta behind to join them on their journey. A life-journey without Vedanta always leads to a dead-end. This is because one is not clear that the pursuit of the infinite is indeed the pursuit of oneself. Since the self is already infinite, it is an as-though pursuit. No matter what one pursues in life, one is looking for oneself as limitless and whole. In the process of understanding this one takes many detours and, with great grace, one finally arrives at the right place. You have been there. You have done that.

You have met many dead-ends and turned back from them repeatedly. Everything in life is a deja vu of sorts. By undergoing a few experiences, one has experienced everything. Take, for example, a holiday. It is like any other holiday. There will be mountains, or there will be water, or there will be woods, or a combination thereof.

That is why, with some enquiry it becomes easy to allow things to drop away. The first thing to let go is unnecessary interaction. I think it is unnecessary to define what an unnecessary interaction is, because everyone knows what it is like when engaged in something unnecessary. You know in your heart this is not needed. You recognize that you need to get out of it, ASAP. When these distractions go, you can heal the reasons behind seeking these distractions. This is the pursuit of *mokṣa*.

The desire for studying Vedanta exponentially grows when needless things are dropped, because you have made the space for it. In other words, you give yourself the present self-abidance. Abidance in oneself is Vedanta.

Chapter 16
PERSON OF SELF-KNOWLEDGE

Conduct of a Jñānin

Question: How does a *vidvān*, a person of self-knowledge, as referred to in *ānandam brahmaṇo vidvān*, go about leading life? How do people see this *vidvān*?

Answer: A *vidvān*, a person of self-knowledge, leads life just as anyone else would. For example, when hungry, they eat, when thirsty, they drink, and when tired, they rest. There is a tendency to spiritually romanticize a person of self-knowledge like Arjuna did in the Bhagavad-Gita. It takes time for this spiritual idealization of the *jñānin* to fade.

People often have preconceived notions of how a *jñānin* should look or behave, even though self-knowledge has nothing to do with appearances or tastes.

In the *Chāndogyopaniṣad*, there is a story about a Vedanta teacher whose name was Raikva, and who did not fit the stereotypical image of an enlightened person.

One King Janaśruti made up his mind to study with the best Vedanta teacher that he could find. Being a king, he thought that he could summon anyone he liked to his palace and make them teach him. He sent his ministers in all directions to scour the kingdom and ordered them to bring him the best *vidvān*. After making enquiries, the ministers came to know that of all the teachers, Raikva was the best.

Finding Raikva was not easy. The ministers could not have his GPS coordinates, so they had to search the dense forest thoroughly for days on end. Finally, they found Raikva sitting under a broken-down chariot. Clad in tatters, he had a severe skin ailment and was busy scratching himself all over and plucking at the scabs– an appearance designed to repel even the most determined seekers. Upon being requested to accompany the ministers to the palace, Raikva plainly refused. The king's men were forced to return without him and report their findings to Janaśruti. Accompanied by elephants laden with gifts and gold, Janaśruti himself approached Raikva and asked for *brahmavidyā*.

Our stereotypical idea of a *jñānin* does not match Raikva in appearance or behavior. We must commend King Janaśruti, who, despite Raikva's appearance, did not flee in disgust, and managed to ask for the teachings.

The point of this story is that there is no specific appearance or behavior that defines a person of self-knowledge. This leads to the second part of the question: How do we recognize a *vidvān*?

Often, we do not even realize we are in the presence of a *vidvān*, because only a *vidvān* can recognize another *vidvān*. A person who is not a *vidvān* cannot recognize one.

Further, *vidvāns* do not advertise their self-knowledge. They do not wear a badge proclaiming their erudition. Why would they? Since one is already fulfilled and content, there is no sense of lack or insecurity centered on the self. Therefore, there is no need to seek validation from others. A *vidvān* would feel no need to announce, "Hey everyone! I have self-knowledge." A *vidvān* remains quiet about any achievements. Consequently, people may not understand that they are in the presence of a *vidvān*.

The knowledgeable ones move through life quietly. A celebrated Vedanta text known as *Vivekacūḍāmaṇi* says:

> **शान्ता महान्तो निवसन्ति सन्तः। वसन्तवल्लोक हितं चरन्तः॥ तीर्णाः स्वयं भीमभवार्णवं जनान्। अहेतुना अन्यानपि तारयन्तः॥**
>
> ***śāntā mahānto nivasanti santaḥ* I**
> ***vasantavalloka hitam carantaḥ* II**
> ***tīrṇa svayam bhīmabhavārṇam janān* I**
> ***ahetunānyānapi tārayantaḥ* II**
>
> Peaceful and magnanimous saints live in the world. Like the spring season, they move around doing good to people. Having themselves crossed the fearful ocean of *saṃsāra*, they help others also cross for no reason at all. II VC 37 II

If asked to teach or answer questions, they will, but otherwise, they live their lives like anyone else.

Addressing the question of how to find a guru, The Upanishads provide the criteria for selecting a teacher. The first criterion given by the Upanishads is to choose a *śrotriya*. This is discernible. A *śrotriya* is someone who has studied within a proper lineage that does not distort the message of the Upanishads. For instance, they do not twist the sentence "*Tat tvam asi*" into "*Atat tvam asi*," implying "you are not Brahman." Some people teach this distortion.

The correct teaching is: "*Sa ātmā tat tvam asi*, Śvetaketo." In Sanskrit, due to its structure, "*ātmā*" with long "ā" and "*tat tvam asi*" can be misinterpreted as "*ātmā atat tvam asi*," suggesting- you are separate from everything!

Do I need to study the Upanishads for 12 years under a teacher only to be told at the end that I am separate from everything else? I already knew that before, and the discomfort with this sense of separation lead me to seek an ashram!

Therefore, *śrotriya* means someone who comes from a sound lineage, and that is the first criterion. The other one is *brahmaniṣṭha*, which means being committed to and constantly abiding in Brahman. No one can know what a *jñānin* is thinking. Are they contemplating upon Brahman or constantly thinking about chocolate cake? You cannot find out. Therefore, we heavily rely on the first criterion.

Question: Is the *vidvān* fearless?

Answer: A *vidvān* is indeed fearless, but this should be understood properly. For example, if a *vidvān* is walking in a mountainous region and there is a landslide, will the *vidvān* run away, or not? Fearlessness does not mean that the *vidvān* will stand there and be crushed under the boulder when escape is clearly possible. That would be foolishness, not fearlessness. The *vidvān* might run away even before you do! This action does not make them any less of a *vidvān* or less fearless.

But then you might wonder, knowing that the landslide is *vyavahārika,* part of the empirical reality, the *vidvān* should remain in the absolute reality, *paramārthika,* at all times.

It is important to understand that while the landslide is *mithyā*, the act of running away from the landslide is also *mithyā*. Therefore it does not negate a *vidvān's* understanding or their fearlessness.

Mithyā landslide, *mithyā* running, *mithyā* hunger, and *mithyā* food– all are part of the empirical reality. *Mithyā* is the empirical or dependent reality. There is no *mithyā* without *satya*, which is you, consciousness. Therefore, fearlessness is not foolishness.

Fearlessness means that a *vidvān* is not emotionally shaken by any challenges that come their way. Challenges will come, as they also have a body like everyone else. A *vidvān's* body also ages and is subject to disease and death.

We often hear that the cause of many diseases, like hypertension or high blood pressure, is stress. If a *vidvān* has high blood pressure, does that mean they are stressed out? Not necessarily. Regardless of how well one takes care of the body, it will eventually deteriorate.

The body is just like a car– no matter how well you take maintain it, it will eventually fall apart. Why? Because it has its own "cār…ma." If it is car trouble, you call it "kārma"; otherwise, it is simply pronounced as karma.

Anything that is put together will eventually come apart. This does not mean you should not maintain the body. You should take care of it, eat all the antioxidant berries you want, and do whatever it takes. But despite all efforts, the body will still deteriorate. It is important to be realistic about this. When there is pain in the body a *vidvān* does not let it morph into mental anguish, fear, or sorrow. That is the key distinction between the one who has the vision of Vedanta and the one who does not.

Question: Can you tell us about your day?

There is nothing much to tell. I am just a regular person. I do the same things you do. I eat, drink, go for a walk, and teach in between. I study books. I am a very ordinary person. It is my Guru who is extraordinary. It is studying at his feet that is extraordinary. That today I teach, that this knowledge works, and that he speaks through all his students is indeed extraordinary. Although he may have left his body, he is very much present here, everywhere, all the time. That is extraordinary. That is the miracle.

Question: You and other teachers have so much knowledge and your memories are amazing! I just wonder about us. How do we get there? Where do we even start? That is the question.

Answer: You do not need to memorize things to have self-knowledge. As soon as I said that everybody started to look suddenly relieved! You do not need to memorize; you just need to listen with an open heart, giving the *śāstra* the benefit of the doubt. If you want to teach, some memorization is necessary, but if you just want *mokṣa*, you do not need to memorize.

Memorizing will not do any good in that sense. If you memorize the expression, "I am Brahman," and rock back and forth, it will not help. You have to understand that. When you relax and listen, you remember more than if you force yourself to do so. It is not about the mind engaging itself; the mind is a servant of this knowledge. It should stand at the door, asking, "What can I do? How can I be of service?" The mind is a receptacle where knowledge is received, and that is why we spend so much time preparing the mind to be tranquil and receptive.

There is a joke from the 70s. A *brahmacārin* went to a householder because he wanted live kindling to cook some *khichari* for himself. The lady of the house said, "Sure, I will give you the kindling. What did you bring to receive the coals?" He replied, "I have a newspaper." She said, "Are you out of your mind? You are going to walk all the way back, carrying live coal in a newspaper? It will just burn. Not only will the newspaper be destroyed, but you will also be hurt. No use. Go get a metal container."

Likewise, if the mind is flimsy, unprepared, and unfocused, and is unable to make the simplest of decisions, then, the mind must be strengthened through meditation.

We learn to make decisions and live with the consequences. Oh, but what if there is FOMO

– fear of missing out? Live with it. Live with the discomfort. What if I make a mistake? Live with the consequences. Living with the results of action makes one grow to be more responsible and accountable. The idea is to train the mind repeatedly, thoroughly and gently.

Training the mind is just like going to the gym. One day, you do a few bench-presses and then look in the mirror for a muscle– nothing. The second day, still no muscle. The third day, no muscle. After one month, a baby muscle starts popping up on the arm. This is how we have to train the mind.

The mind must be kept on a steady diet of devotion, service, and listening to the Upanishads. It has to continuously surrender to listening, and only then everything goes in. This is what you need to really assimilate this knowledge and be free of sorrow and fear. You do not need anything else. Memorization is necessary only if you want to teach it to others, but not otherwise.

Chapter 17
THE THREE BODIES

Question: The question is about the causal body. You did not say much about the causal body, and then you said we are not any of these three bodies. Can you expand on this?

Answer: The causal body is self-ignorance. The causal body is the cause of birth, which is *ātma-ajñāna*. Self-ignorance is not knowing oneself as Brahman, as whole, limitless and free of the notions of bondage. Therefore, if one is ignorant of oneself, one comes to many wrong conclusions. Consequently, one comes to think of oneself variously, as identified with the body etc., which are incorrect. These incorrect assimilations of "I," and that is what leads to birth. That is what leads to baggage, and the cause of all this is the causal body.

If I say I am the physical body, then what happens? One is fraught with fear, always afraid. Oh, what is going to happen now? Oh, one more gray hair, one more wrinkle! Oh, one more joint is not working.

A little analysis makes it clear that one is not the body. One survives the body. And one is obviously not the subtle body either. The subtle body is composed of seventeen elements, including desires that are carried from life to life for no extra charge. We know we are not our luggage, yet there is an identification with the subtle body.

I was traveling with someone and, having reached our destination, we were waiting for the luggage to arrive. The carousel was going around, and when my co-traveler saw her bag, she got very excited. Pointing to the suitcase, she exclaimed, "That's me, that's me!" I said, "No, that is not you, that is just your suitcase."

You are not the causal body because the cause of birth is self-ignorance. Although we speak a lot about self-ignorance, it is important to remember that we are talking of the ignorance of the self on part of the *jīva*; we are not saying that the self is ignorant. The self is totally free of ignorance. Even to say "I am self-ignorant," I have to *know* that I do not know myself.

If I am not any of these bodies, and I cannot say that I am non-existent, then what am I? The answer is *saccidānanda*, Brahman. I am *Īśvara* in the form of awareness, full, present, limitless consciousness that never comes to an end.

This consciousness is "as though" sporting a physical body, a subtle body, a causal body, "as though" sporting the mind, "as though" sporting a house, a spouse, a life. When you know the *satya*, the truth of yourself, all the *mithyā* world, this world of dependent reality, becomes a play. When you know the truth, you can have fun. You can play. Otherwise, you take the game too seriously.

Intellect

Question: My question relates to our layers of existence. You referred to the body-mind complex. So, there is the body, the mind, the intellect, the memory, the ego, and the self. There was a time when I thought everything was intellect because the intellect pays my bills. I did not even know that there was more than that. I think the majority of humanity is caught in a bubble called intellect or mind. Can you talk about that?

Answer: The world is very heady these days. In fact, you have said it beautifully; I am not sure what else I can add to it. It is easier to give up body-identification, but it is extremely difficult to understand that one is not the mind. There is a *Taittirīyopaniṣad* mantra:

> **यतो वाचो निवर्तन्ते । अप्राप्य मनसा सह ॥**
>
> *yato vāco nivartante* I *aprāpya manasā saha* II
>
> From which cause, not having gained Brahman, speech turns back along with the mind.
>
> II TU 2.9.1 II

The mind having failed to objectify Brahman beats a sad little retreat along with its friend, the speech. Speech and mind, of course, are the best of friends; each slightly envious of the other. The mind says to speech, "Oh, you are so flowery; you can put into words all my thoughts, thank you." Speech says, "I am so envious; you think of such amazing things. You are so creative. Let us be friends and set the world on fire."

The mind and speech can wax eloquent about everything in the universe, but when they set forth to describe Brahman, the truth of the self, they just return with their heads hung low. They had to say, "We have failed. We are not successful in this mission of objectifying Brahman." As soon as the mind tries to conceptualize Brahman in any form or name or categorize Brahman, it is gone; it loses itself. Because Brahman is not a category, it is you.

Brahman is not a noun; it is not a verb. It does not do anything and has no relationship to anything, because it is the only thing there is. It is not *jāti* or *guṇa*. Since it does not have attributes, it cannot be described with adjectives. Therefore, the mind and speech must retreat. In fact, to know this is to surrender. The enactment of this surrender is in the form of a *namaskāra,* where the whole body bends down. In this bending, the mind loses its way. When it returns, it is more tranquil and receptive. When this happens, there is a lot of space for this teaching to be absorbed. Otherwise, there is no room for the teaching.

There is another Zen master story, similar to the one narrated earlier. A man repeatedly kept asking a Zen master to teach him. The master kept replying, "Not today." This went on for several days. Finally, the man asked, "Why are you not teaching me?" The master asked him to bring a glass of water. The man obliged. The master then took some mud from the ground, put it in the water, and stirred it until it was completely turbid. "This is the state of the mind" said the master. Then he suggested they go for a walk. When they returned after half an hour, the mud had settled to the bottom, leaving the water clear. The master said, "When your mind is like this, I can teach you."

The mind is full of itself, getting in its own way and tripping all over itself. It wants to know but will not sit still. It is a great friend of speech on one side and the *ahaṅkāra* on the other, and all these mischief-mongers hinder the assimilation of knowledge.

This is why we have to practice *japa* and *sevā*. For cleaning the body, we have soap that we use regularly. *Japa* is the soap for cleaning the *antaḥkaraṇa*, the mind. Each *mantra* is like a brand of soap for inner cleansing. *Mantra-japa* makes the mind peaceful and free of distractions. *Japa* bestows the mind with the *prasāda* of *cittanaiścalya*, steadfastness and focus.

Sevā is not merely fulfilling a duty; it is transforming the heart enough to go out and give. *Karmayoga* and *sevā* take care of neutralizing *rāga-dveṣa,* bringing purification, *cittaśuddhi,* in their wake. They purify the mind and make it free of grudges, complaints, and resentment. This is how the mind is prepared.

We must shed the analytical aspect of the mind. However, we still need the mind to study, so it is brought in as a servant through the back door. Initially, the mind thinks it is the king, sitting on the throne. We take away its crown and make it a servant, allowing it to sit and listen. It is not the author of *brahmavidyā*. Knowledge happens in the mind; but not by the mind.

Question: Swaminiji, can I have a follow-up on the same topic? Sometimes you hear, "I am not my body, I am not my mind, I am not the ego," but when you say that while inside a bubble, that bubble is called intellect. How do you burst the bubble known as the intellect. How can we use the intellect to get past the intellect?

Answer: The *Nirvāṇaṣaṭkam* says, *"mano-budhyahaṅkāra-cittāni nāham.* I am not the mind, or the intellect or the *ahaṅkāra* or the emotions.

Question: But then I am still in a bubble. Does intellect talk to intellect?

Answer: You are not the intellect; you are using the intellect as the pole in the pole vault game. You run along with a long pole and use it as a leverage to go over a rope, by sticking the pole in the sand. Then what happens to the pole? It just drops. You do not carry it with you to the other side. Likewise, you are using the mind and intellect as leverage to reach the place of being the *sākṣin*, the observer.

The intellect is a place where knowledge happens, but it is not the agent of the knowledge. This is because the knowledge is not of a finite object that needs to be brought to light by the intellect. The knowledge is non-separate from you the self, which cannot be objectified. Moreover, being self-evident, the self need not be objectified. Just like in the pole vault, you use the intellect up to a point, after which there is no need for it anymore.

The last line of the verse from the *Nirvāṇaṣaṭkam* says this clearly: *cidānandarūpaḥ śivo'ham. śivo'ham*– I am that which is consciousness, *ānanda*, limitlessness, and *śiva*. auspiciousness. *Śiva* means pure and auspicious. I am free of regret and hurt. I am free of all karma. This is why I am *śiva*. In oneness, there is no place for the intellect to stand out separately.

Chapter 18
MISCELLANEOUS

Mantras and Scriptures

Question: Regarding *Brahmānanda-Valli,* I got confused about the mind and intellect. Please explain.

Answer:

> यतो वाचो निवर्तन्ते। अप्राप्य मनसा सह॥
>
> *yato vāco nivartante* I *aprāpya manasā saha* II
>
> From which causeless cause the mind and the speech retreat, having not gained (Brahman as an object.II TU 2.9.1 II

This means "Where the mind and speech retreat, unable to grasp the *ātman* as an object." The idea is that *ātman* is not an object.

For instance, objects like a paper clip, a piece of paper, or a microphone can be perceived and understood using the usual means of knowledge. However, the "I" is not an object.

It is not tangible; it has no name or form. *Ātman* is a term we use to indicate that which does not have form, color, taste, hands, legs, movement, or activity. It does not perform any actions. Thus, it is impossible to objectify the *ātman*. Because of this, the mind, which categorizes everything, ultimately gives up, and speech, which converts thoughts into articulate expressions, also retreats. That is what this line means. It indicates that *ātman* must be understood in a different way, not as an object but as the very essence oneself that is beyond our usual modes of understanding.

Question: Please explain the word "*pratipakṣa-bhāvana*" and how it operates in our thinking. I am also confused about the meaning of the word "*samatva*" and whether these concepts come into conflict.

Answer: The term *pratipakṣa-bhāvana* comes from Patanjali's Yoga Sutra:

> वितर्कबाधने प्रतिपक्षभावनम् ॥
> *vitarka-*
> *bādhanepratipakṣabhāvanam* II
> When improper thoughts hinder, take
> the opposite stance II YS 2.33 II

It means adopting the opposite stance of whatever emotion one is feeling at any given point in time. For example, if one has thoughts about harming another, one changes the trajectory of the thoughts to have compassion for the person.

The other word you mentioned, *samatva* means equanimity in receiving *karmaphala*, fruits of action. These concepts are not contradictory. You might feel a certain way, like wanting to say something angrily to the person who cut the line in front of you at the grocery shop. However, you do not follow through. Instead, you practice *pratipakṣa-bhāvanā* by taking the opposite stance. You try to see that although person's behavior was rude, perhaps he or she was in a hurry. You practice patience and compassion, which are the opposite of anger. This is not contradictory to doing what needs to be done or maintaining equanimity– they are actually aligned.

Equanimity is a core aspect of *karmayoga*. One definition of yoga is:

> **योगस्थः कुरु कर्माणि सङ्गं त्यक्त्वा धनञ्जय।**

सिद्ध्यसिद्ध्योः समो भूत्वा समत्वं योग उच्यते॥

yogasthaḥ kuru karmāṇi
saṅgaṃ tyaktvā dhanañjaya ।
siddhyasiddhyoḥ samo bhūtvā
samatvaṁ yoga ucyate ॥ *BG 2.48* ॥

Yoga is maintaining equanimity, especially in receiving the results of actions. Equanimity in yoga does not mean being passive in action but rather being balanced in accepting their outcomes. By not getting excessively elated when things go well, you reduce the severity of distress when things do not go as planned. This cultivation of equanimity is a salient precursor to attaining self-knowledge.

Question: I have always been curious about the meaning of the *pūrṇamadaḥ mantraḥ*. Can you speak about it?

Answer:

ओम् पूर्णमदः पूर्णमिदं पूर्णात् पूर्णमुदच्यते।
पूर्णस्य पूर्णमादाय पूर्णमेवावशिष्यते॥
ओम् शान्तिः शान्तिः शान्तिः॥

Oṁ pūrṇamadaḥ Pūrṇamidaṃ pūrṇāt
pūrṇamudacyate । *pūrṇasya pūrṇamādāya*
pūrṇamevāvaśiṣyate ॥ *Oṁ śāntiḥ śāntiḥ Śāntiḥ* ॥

> The cause is whole, the effect (the *jagat*) is also whole. When the whole comes from the whole, what remains is the whole. II *Śukla-Yajurveda śāntimantra* II

The word *"adas,"* means "that." *Idam* means "this." The word "that" in the tradition, is always used as a shorthand for Brahman, *Īśvara*, God, because it is not something that is easily understood and, therefore, it appears to be remote, not locally available. This is our thinking, which is actually a misunderstanding. Therefore, the Upanishad goes along with our self-ignorance and, for the time-being says "that" is *pūrṇa*.

Pūrṇa means that which is whole in every way. Even though the word "whole" is just a word, here it means much more than "not half." Here, whole means limitless. This is what one wants to be. When one says one wants to feel happy, it means one wants to feel whole. One wants to feel secure means one wants to feel whole. Nowadays, there is a big hype about holistic health and wholesome food. The word "whole" has an abiding presence in our conversations because it resonates with everyone. So, *pūrṇa* means that which is complete, which does not need anything else to complete it.

This is a far cry from one's experience of everyday life, where waking up does not happen without a cup of coffee to complete the person. The talk among the Sivananda ashram visitors is, "Oh no, there is no coffee served here. OMG! Let us quickly locate the nearest Starbucks via GPS." I get messages on the phone, too: "Swaminiji, we am going to Starbucks. Can we get you a latte?" and I respond by saying, "It is a little '*latte*' for that." We are dependent on an aid to wake us up, and then we need an aid to put us to sleep.

In between the waking and the sleep states, there are countless props needed. At every step of the way, one needs to be validated and told that they are okay. When that does not happen– when the opposite happens– and one faces criticism instead, one needs a big chocolate bar to stuff down the pain. That is why, I suppose in Western countries, there are vending machines dispensing chips, chocolates, and soda practically at every street corner. Then after having chocolate for breakfast, there is a feeling of guilt. To assuage the guilt, one needs another prop– perhaps one will browse the internet to find an article that says that dark chocolate is therapeutic for the heart. *Ayyo!* Where is one to go? We have not even got through half of the day yet. Even talking about this is dizzying in all its implications.

They say it takes a whole village to raise a child, but it does not end there. It takes the entire universe to prop up just one adult! So many needs one has– a bustle of needs from day to night. Therefore, it is not a surprise that one thinks, "I am not whole. I feel like Swiss cheese full of holes, but not whole."

Pūrṇa means the cause. The cause from which everything has come is whole. This is a sentence in the Upanishad. This means the manifest universe, starting with this fragile body, which is prone to falls, aging, disease, and death– is still whole, because it comes from a source that is whole. Being Brahman, the cause, is whole. The effect, which is this manifest universe starting with our own bodies, shares the same DNA as *Bhagavān*. What is the DNA of *Bhagavān*? *Saccidānanda* is *Bhagavān's* DNA, and so it is also the *jīva's* DNA. This is how it is.

We share that same wholeness of the cause. The effect cannot be separate from the cause. From an oak tree, you cannot expect to get coconuts. Similarly, from *saccidānanda*, which is whole, free, and limitless, you cannot expect to get something finite or limited. It just cannot happen. So, *pūrṇamadaḥ pūrṇamidam*– from that whole came this whole.

Then, of course, there might be a question: when *Bhagavān* manifested as this universe, one might think that *saccidānanda* got very slim and disappeared. If that is the raw material of the universe, it should disappear, like spreading some butter on a slice of bread. Soon the butter is all gone. No, it is whole, meaning it never comes to an end. It is always the same, unchanging limitlessness, free of depletion. That is the wholeness, which is the manifest universe, non-separate from God.

When *Bhagavān* manifested in the form of this variegated infinite universe of infinite names and forms, *saccidānanda-Bhagavān* did not undergo any change, because *Bhagavān* is infinite, whole, and free, that is what it means.

Pūrṇasya pūrṇamādāya pūrṇameva avaśiṣyate–When you take away the whole from the whole, what remains is the whole, because it is a projected universe, non-separate from *Bhagavān*.

For example, if you dream of spending a lot of money, are you poorer the next morning? No, your financial portfolio is intact. The dream spending is just a projection of your memory and desires, that is all. When we talk of the *samaṣṭi,* the total, it is *Bhagavān*'s memory of the previous cycle of creation, and all the *jīvas'* desires, which are one with *Bhagavān*.

Jīva means a crazy person, one who complains a lot, okay? Tell anybody this, and they will agree with you that *jīvas* are crazy. We do not know what we are doing. First, we say, "O Lord, I want to be one with you. I am crying for you, when will you give me darshan? Please come, take me. Swing low, sweet chariot, come forth and carry me home. Why am I away from you? Let me in!" And *Bhagavān* takes these desires seriously and says, "Okay, come along, be one with me," and then there is *pralaya*, the resolution of the universe.

For some time the *jīva* is contented, but the force of an unfulfilled agenda quickens the desire to have a body again, akin to the unborn baby kicking in the mother's womb. The *jīva* then says "Let me out! I want to be on my own. I want to be independent. I do not want to be one with you. It is so boring being *saccidānanda* all the time. You do not do anything. There are no movies, malls, or friends. There is no drama, there is only Rāma. I want to be me. I want to see what I can do. I have places to go, people to see, and things to do. Let me out. I want a body to fulfill my desires; I want a world to interact with." *Bhagavān* said "Tathāstu" and the universe came into being again. Did the *jīva* stop complaining? On the contrary, the complaints only increased.

That is why *Bhagavān* talks very little because he has to deal with our insanity on a daily basis. *Bhagavān* does not need cable TV. Every *jīva* is a reality channel. Vishnu says, "Whatever you want. You want to be free? Go, I will create another universe, and you can stomp around and exhaust your karma."

"Can I be born again?"

"Sure, because you will have so many desires, you will have to be born again. Go for it, be born again and again and again." This is how it is. *Bhagavān* does not undergo any change at all. The universe is non-separate from *Bhagavān* even when it is manifest. That is why we say every tree is *Bhagavān*. In fact, every tree is worshiped in India, and they even arrange marriages between two trees. Sometimes two trees grow intertwined like in *garuḍāsana*. Then the villagers come and perform a very elaborate marriage ceremony for the trees.

This is *pūrṇa*. Everything is *pūrṇa* because everything is *Bhagavān*. In fact, even our desserts are called *pūrṇa*. The stuffing, the sweet filling, is called *pūrṇa*. You take some bland dough like rice flour or wheat flour, and fill it with the *pūrṇa*– a stuffing of coconut and jaggery– and then you steam or fry it. This dish is called *modaka* and is made for *Gaṇeśacaturthī* Lord Ganesha's festival. As children, we used to remove the outer skin of the *modaka*, throw it away, and eat only the filling. Everybody wants only the *pūrṇa*. See that? Even our sweet dishes are Vedantic!

Question: Swaminiji, I was trying to understand *Īśvarārpaṇa-buddhi* and would appreciate some tips to put it into action.

Answer: *Īśvarārpaṇa-buddhi* means an attitude of dedicating all that one does to *Īśvara*.

> **यत्करोषि यदश्नासि यज्जुहोषि ददासि यत्।**
> **यत्तपस्यसि कौन्तेय तत्कुरुष्व मदर्पणम्॥**
> ***yatkaroṣi yadaśnasi yad juhoṣi dadasi yat*** **।**
> ***yattapasyasi kaunteya tattat kuruṣva madarpaṇam*** **॥**
>
> Whatever you do, whatever you eat, whatever you offer, whatever you give in charity, whatever tapas you practice, O Kaunteya, do it as an offering to me. ॥ BG 9.27 ॥

Īśvarārpaṇa cannot be developed without first cultivating relationship with *Īśvara*. All this we have been talking about. To put this into action we pray with intention and make the prayer real. In the beginning, it may not feel real, especially if one is not accustomed to praying. You may feel like you are faking it, but actually, you are not. Sometimes it feels like you are talking to yourself. In truth, you are talking to the highest aspect of yourself. We make it real. Do whatever it takes to enact that. It is an enactment of a relationship, and it is real– it is the primary relationship. It is the relationship of reclaiming your identity as a devotee.

The *bhakta* is the primary identity, and when that is in place, you can be a devotee son, a devotee daughter, a devotee husband, a devotee wife, a devotee mom, a devotee dad, a devotee employer, a devotee employee, a devotee *karmayogin*. The word "devotee" is always in front of all the roles you play, because when your connection to the source is right, you are alright with everything. So that is what one has to do. After that, it becomes habitual to offer all of one's actions to *Bhagavān*.

Question: What is the name of your organization. Can you speak on its meaning?

Answer: My guru, Pujya Swamiji gave the name Arsha Vijnana Gurukulam. "Arṣa" is a noun, which means that which comes from the *ṛṣis*. *Vijñāna* means knowledge, specifically the well-ascertained, well-established knowledge of the self. *Jñāna* alone means knowledge, but *vijñāna* signifies a deeper, more precise understanding *Gurukula* is a place where one studies while living with the teacher.

Chanting

Question: I have a question about *ślokas* and *stotras*. Yesterday, you said that we need to pronounce them correctly. Growing up, we learned many *ślokas*, and I know I do not say them properly. Does that mean it was a waste? Is there a good way to start? Should we start with the pronunciations first and then learn them? I just wanted to understand the process.

Answer: Pronunciation is part of learning. Once you know your pronunciations are incorrect, correct them. Rectify those mistakes, then learn new ones. You can learn new ones at the same time, no problem.

This is a true story. A small child went to play-school and came back. The mother asked the child, "What did they teach you today at school?" The child replied, "Hopeless Mommy, hopeless Daddy, hopeless teachers, hopeless friends." The mother said, "What is this? Repeat it again." The child said, "Hopeless, hopeless, hopeless." The mother wondered what was going on in the school and went to the teacher with a complaint: "What are you teaching the children?"

Upon hearing what the child was saying the teacher burst out laughing. He clarified that he had taught the children to pray "Oh bless mommy, oh bless daddy, oh bless teachers, and oh bless friends." The three year old had heard it as "hopeless." Do you think this child would have accrued bad karma from chanting it like that for a few days? No, because the child did not know any better.

Similarly, we may be saying many things incorrectly, but until we know, it is all forgiven.

Customs, Rituals, and Affirmations

Question: **We have the Vedantic path and the path that includes customs that you follow as part of the family. What is the difference?**

Answer: Customs and rituals are preparation for the study of Vedanta. They help to prepare the mind to neutralize the *rāga-dveṣa*, and develop *bhakti*, devotion.

When we do *pūjā,* we learn to sit without complaining for a couple of hours. That is a very good practice, as it increases the *titikṣā* threshold. This is all *sādhana*. There is only one path, namely, to understand that I am already what I seek. How you go on this path is up to you, whether you commit to it full time, or commit to it while also fulfilling other desires at the same time. That is the only difference. *Bhakti* is common to both paths.

Question: There are some customs around the solar and lunar eclipses. Do you want to elaborate on that? Does it affect us?

Answer: Yes, it has an effect. Everything has an effect, because in the *jagat* everything is connected. There are certain customs. For example, a common custom is fasting during the eclipse. Then you might ask, "Why should not I eat? What is the connection between the shadow of the earth falling on the sun and me not eating?" Intermittent fasting is popular now, but in ancient India, we practiced it regularly.

Every *Ekādaśī,* the eleventh day of the waning and waxing moon, there is only one meal. Once a week, you might have only one meal, depending on horoscopic deficiencies. For example, if you have a retrograde Jupiter in the chart, you need his grace, so you fast on a Thursday. If Śukra, Venus, is debilitated, you fast on a Friday because you do not want Lakshmi to go away from you. One or two weekly fasts might already be there, plus a fortnightly fast, and some festivals will also include fasting. These fasts are all ways of detoxing and cleansing the body.

People often focus on what they should not do and forget what they should do. What we should do during an eclipse is *japa*. Eclipses are very good for meditation. When you meditate during an eclipse, it is incredibly powerful. Try it, you will like it.

An eclipse is seen as a pollutant due to ultraviolet rays coming into the house. Generally no one goes outside during either an eclipse, especially a solar eclipse, and the curtains are drawn in the house to block out the sun's rays. All the food cooked before the eclipse is thrown away; you do not eat it after the eclipse. This practice is a form of spiritual discipline.

In the Hindu tradition, like in the Jewish tradition, there is a strong focus on cleanliness and avoiding pollutants. The concepts of purity and pollution are very prominent in both traditions. I respect that. Whether we know the meaning of it or not, it is important not to mix certain things, even in food. You would not eat certain things together. There are also ritual baths in addition to everyday bathing for special occasions, emphasizing purification.

Question: Swaminiji, I read about affirmations. How can you bring affirmations into our path for building self-awareness?

Answer: Affirmations can be very powerful, especially when you write your own. They are more effective than when someone else writes them for you. For example, if the affirmation is about a body-image issue, you might write "Hello, beautiful," and post it on the mirror. Look at it every day without skepticism. Simply look at it and absorb the message.

You can also use affirmations from the Upanishads. For instance, if you find yourself in a sticky situation, you can say, "*asaṅgo'ham, asaṅgo'ham, asango'haṃ punaḥ punaḥ*. I am *saccidānanda*. I am *saccidānanda*." This means, "I am not affected by this. I can extricate myself from this." If someone is sinking into depression, they can repeat, "*ānando'ham*," meaning "I am *ānanda*." Making this a daily practice is a very good *sādhana*.

Question: We learn from the Upanishads that many *gurus* and *ṛṣis* were householders. Yet today, it seems that most gurus are Swamis. Does this mean that to gain self-knowledge, one must become a renunciant?

Answer: This is not necessary. There are two traditions in Vedanta: the *gṛhastha-paramparā,* the lineage of householders, and that of *sannyāsis,* the renunciants. It is quite interesting because there is often a silent competition between these two lifestyles. Each group tends to see itself as better than the other. Vyāsa, one of the most revered figures in Vedanta, was a family man.

Vyāsa was married and led a householder's life. In contrast, his son, Śuka, left home at the age of five. I imagine that he did not speak much, but when he finally did, his first words might have been, "Bye mom, bye dad." His parents would have said, "What? You still need us! you are just five." Śuka might have replied, "Hmmm. I do not think I need you."

His parents would have then pleaded, "Okay, okay, let us rephrase that. We need you. Do not go!" But Śuka left anyway. As he departed, he offered his grieving parents a boon: "Whenever you think of me, whenever you need me, I will be here." True to his word, he would often appear in the form of a parrot, which is why he was called Śuka.

The *Muṇḍakopaniṣad* enumerates this detail:

> **ओम् ब्रह्मा देवानां प्रथमः सम्बभूव विश्वस्यकर्ता**
> **भुवनस्य गोप्ता। स ब्रह्मविद्यां सर्वविद्याप्रतिष्ठाम्**
> **अथर्वाय ज्येष्ठपुत्राय प्राह॥**
> ***Oṁ brahmā devānāṃ prathamaḥ***
> ***saṃbabhūva viśvasya kartā bhuvanasya goptā ।***
> ***sa brahmavidyāṃ sarvavidyāpratiṣṭhām atharvāya***
> ***jyeṣṭhaputrāya prāha ॥***
>
> Lord Brahmaji, the creator and sustainer of the worlds, was the first among the devas. He imparted *brahmavidyā*, the source of all knowledge, to his eldest son, Atharva.
>
> ॥ MU 1.1.1 ॥

This knowledge was then passed down from Atharva down the lineage. Eventually, we meet our protagonist in the Upanishad, *Śaunaka*, also described as a householder. Why? Because *Śaunaka is* described *as a mahāśāla– mahān śālā yasya saḥ–* the one who has a huge hall for feeding people regularly. The *sannyāsis* neither have a huge hall nor do they feed people. Instead, *sannyāsis* would go to such halls for their food.

In India and, perhaps elsewhere also, many householders gain this knowledge, study, and then teach. While writing the commentary on the *Muṇḍakopaniṣad*, particularly this beginning part, Adi Shankara gives a little caveat. He says, "Please do not think that renunciation has no place in one's life after reading about the *gṛhastha-paramparā.*"

Adi Shankara frequently emphasized *sannyāsa* throughout his works. Wherever possible, he mentioned *sannyāsa*. Academics studying Adi Shankara often note his strong preference for *sannyāsa*, describing him as having a pro-*sannyāsa* bias.

While this may be true, it is also important to understand that to gain self-knowledge, one needs to cultivate the mindset of a renunciant. Even if one is not a practicing renunciant, a dispassionate disposition is essential. The essence of *sannyāsa* is about being a renunciant in spirit, metaphorically dressing the heart in orange robes..

It is not necessary for all gurus to be *sannyāsis*. There are many examples of non-*sannyāsin* gurus who have attained and imparted knowledge, as well as numerous examples of *sannyāsin* gurus.

Question: Can you share a story about Pujya Swamiji? I have heard that you were with him for many years and also had the chance to travel with him. What can you share that will increase our *śraddhā* for this knowledge?

Answer: There are many stories. I can share one from a trip to a village near Rajamundhri. Pujya Swamiji was there for a temple consecration ceremony. The *śraddhā* of the people there was just amazing. It is believed that all the *puṇya,* good karma, of the *jñānīs* goes to their feet. Knowing this, the devotees were literally milking Pujya Swamiji's legs all the way from his knees down to his feet. When scores of people started to do it, we could see that it was painful for him, so we formed a human chain in front of him. This ensured that the people would do *namaskāra* from a distance. Still, some people would sneak in and restart the *puṇya*-milking, if a few of us were slightly distracted.

Just as we thought we had this situation under control, something else happened. They all wanted to put their young babies in Swamiji's lap to get his blessings. But when the *mahātman* is so far away and there is a teeming mass of devotees, what do you do? How do you get your baby blessed? I guess desperate situations call for desperate measures. The villagers thought that the only option is to hoist the baby above the shoulders and simply fling it in the direction of the *mahātman*, which is exactly what they all started to do.

Oh my God! They all had so much *śraddhā* that the baby would be caught and placed in Swamiji's lap and then returned back to its parents. So many babies were flung about, that at one point it was raining babies, and we were all frantically trying to catch them. Now I feel like adding the disclaimer frequently found in films: No babies were harmed during this exercise! That no babies got dropped was truly a miracle. It was *śraddhā* absolute. It was beautiful and transformative sight.

One of my *gurubhais* said, "I wish I had this kind of *śraddhā;* I would have understood Vedanta a long time ago." We also joked about how the expression "it just fell into my lap" might have originated from this kind of an incident.

Ahimsā and Vegetarianism

Question: **I have been reading the Bible and I wonder about the offerings of animals and the eating of meat. It seems like a contradiction because, in the Hindu tradition, we practice *ahimsā*. Yet, Jesus, who did no harm and but ate meat. How do you reconcile this?**

Answer: I do not know if you need to reconcile it. The word "dominion" is not present in our teachings. The Bible says one has dominion over everything that flies and crawls. I spoke with a few Christian scholars about this subject at some interfaith meeting. They mentioned that in English, "dominion" implies overlordship or power, but in Latin, it means a position of responsibility. It implies that one is responsible for these beings.

We cannot question why Jesus ate fish and meat. During those times, people consumed whatever was available according to their local environment, weather conditions, and customs. Similarly, we cannot go back to the Paleolithic era and tell the caveman not to polish off a yak. That is what was available and known to them at the time. We offer to *Bhagavān* what we eat; offering means giving what we consume. In rural India, there is incidence of animal sacrifice, though it is less prevalent now. In Kali temples, although rare, offerings and *abhiśeka* with animal blood still occur.

We live in an age that is completely different from before. Our *buddhi*, the intellectual faculty, has evolved significantly. It is much more responsive to its environment and needs to be so because the methods of killing animals in Jesus' times are not the same as they are now. There is a big difference.

We often hear stories about cows escaping from slaughterhouses. They sense the tension and danger, so they take the risk of jumping off the truck carrying them to their death. In the past, hunting was different. You went into the forest with a crude knife or with your bare hands, and it was a game of chance: either you became the animal's lunch, or you had the animal for lunch. It was fair game in that sense– sometimes you were lucky, and sometimes the animal prevailed. Now we have all these sophisticated mechanisms of killing; it is unconscionable, really. It is not just about the eating; It is also about how we procure and process what we consume. Therefore, we have to look at things according to the times. That is why now there is an increased focus on vegetarianism. It is a responsible and ethical way of life.

Cultural Appropriation

Question: I have been a yoga teacher for a number of years, and in the past couple of years, I have read about something called cultural appropriation. I have been trying to understand what this means for me as a yoga teacher and as someone who aspires to be authentic. People are saying it is cultural appropriation to take on Sanskrit names, wear Indian clothing, and there is a lot of guilt I feel in terms of what my ancestors did throughout the world. I want to ask for your wisdom on what I can do as a yoga teacher and as a human being to avoid cultural appropriation.

Answer: As a yoga teacher, you are a blessing, and you are erasing, as we speak, so many years of the difficult ancestry you talked about. If you have studied yoga in an authentic place and are practicing it authentically, there is nothing wrong in calling that your occupation. If you want to wear Indian clothes, eat Indian food, and have a Sanskrit name, you have my permission to do that. Have fun!

End of Life

Question: When I was five years old, I watched my mother die, and I was unable to do anything about it. Now, at 58, I have reflected more and more and have decided to become a Death Doula, which means being with people as they pass away. I want to help people find peace as they transition. What advice do you have for someone doing this type of work?

Answer: I applaud you for your decision. It is not an easy decision; it is very difficult. However, this may be where your skill and the source of healing lie, considering what happened when you were five. You are probably already very good at what you do, so any suggestion I can give is just a reinforcement of what you already know. I am just sharing what I think. People are different.

First, I think it is important to connect with the person transitioning. Sometimes people are more or less in a place of acceptance. They may think that they have led a good life and are, more or less, reconciled to their imminent departure. They may still have difficult days, but that does not change the fact that they are generally at peace. They may experience grief, anger, or other emotions, but they are mostly okay. This makes the job easier because you are just being with them, allowing them to live fully on any particular day. You encourage them to live as fully as possible on their own terms, despite their limitations. It is still hard, but it is easier than if you have someone who is not in acceptance. Then things can be very difficult.

Once, a woman who I did not know called me. She got my number through someone and then said, "They say I have stage four cancer. Can you please come and see me?" I went and visited her. The lady told me that the medical establishment said she had only two months to live. So, I asked, "How would you like to spend this time?" Then she said, "I want you to make sure that I do not die." Poor thing! I replied, "I am sorry, but I cannot do that. This is not in our hands."

She insisted, "You are a spiritual leader!" I said, "Well, that is what they say, but that does not mean we have control over matters of birth and death." She then asked me to help her fight all the doctors and everything. I said, "That is not what I do." She asked, "Then what is it that you do?"

I said, "I can chant the Bhagavad-Gita, and it is very soothing. You will listen to it and feel good." As we were discussing this, she wanted to know what the Bhagavad-Gita is. I explained a little, and then her husband walked in. He said, "Oh, is this the one you called?" and she said, "yes."

He then said, "Okay, help me fight the medical establishment, help me keep her alive." I replied, "It is clear you love your wife very much, but I cannot do that. Nobody can do that." He asked, "But are not there miracles?" I said, "We can pray for a miracle, for sure. Anything is possible. You can pray for a miracle." She passed away in less than two months after this incident. It was a very difficult passage, and nothing I could say or do would help. Nothing at all. It is important to recognize this without taking it personally. But that does not in any way detract from your skills, compassion, or how you want the outcome to go.

There might be times when it is in both their best interest and yours to walk away because they may not have accepted the news of the imminent transition. Sometimes people say they have accepted it, but they have not. It is about gauging where the person is and dealing with it at that level. Above all, in the vocation you have chosen, there is a high burnout rate. Guard against that burnout by making plenty of time to rest, recharge, rejuvenate, and to finding joy in small things. You will be surrounded by sad people, so ensure your empathy does not take on their hopelessness or disenchantment. It is easier said than done, but with a strong spiritual practice and plenty of "me time" between visits, I think you will do a fabulous job. I wish you the best!

Question: I teach *yoga-nidra* meditation and would like to guide everyone who is passing

with this method. What do you think of this method for dealing with terminal patients who are nearing their end?

Answer: If the terminally ill people want that, it is a fantastic idea. If they agree and want to do it, go ahead. If they say, "I hate meditation," then you can sing or play some chants. Let them call the shots and let the need come organically from them. If you want to meditate, you can do so anytime, but you cannot expect them to want this particular type of healing. They may not. That is why it is important to go step by step; what works one day may not work the next. Yesterday, they might have meditated, but today, they might not want to hear the word "meditation."

Instead, today, they might want to go for a movie, and tomorrow they might want to do something else, and that is okay. It is scary to look at the end, especially in traditions with no concept of rebirth, where death is seen as the final end. Frequently, this brings up feelings of not having lived life to the fullest. Therefore, it is important to assure them they have done everything properly and to give a lot of validation. When a person is looking at the end of their life, guilt and hurt are the primary emotions. They might feel they have not accomplished something or weren't good enough in some respect. Assuring them that they have achieved a lot, and done everything they could help with a sense of closure. Validating their accomplishments is their meditation on some days.

Question: **I just wanted to know, in your culture, what happens to people who pass away either naturally or unnaturally.**

Answer:

> **योनिमन्ये प्रपद्यन्ते शरीरत्वाय देहिनः।**
> **स्थाणुमन्येऽनुसंयन्ति यथाकर्म यथाश्रुतम्॥**
> *yonimanye prapadyante śarīratvāya dehinaḥ*
> I
> *sthāṇumanye'nusaṃyanti yathākarma*
> *yathāśrutam* II
>
> They (the departed ones) gain other birth canals, while yet others take on forms of trees in keeping their karma and in keeping with the *śāstra*.
>
> II KU 2.2.7 II

This mantra from the *Kaṭhopaniṣad* states that life does not stop at death. This is a universal law. Nothing in the universe comes to an end; it only undergoes transformation. You can burn something, and then you are dealing with ashes. You can bury something, and then you are dealing with compost. It just transforms; it does not really come to an end.

If this is true of all insentient things, what about conscious beings? The Upanishads say that one survives death. The body dies, but the "I" remains. If it is an "I" that is aware of its own glory, then it is *Īśvara*, one with God. It was one with God while that being had a body, and afterwards, it is revered as an *avatāra* of God. But those who do not know the truth of the self seek other birth canals to express themselves, meaning they are born again.

Why are they born again? Because they have excess baggage in a subtle form. All the suitcases full of desires survive death, and since the being is very attached to them, the suitcases are not let go of and merely pass on to the next life. This concept is present not just in Hindu culture but also in Buddhist culture.

There is a book that some of you may be familiar with, called *The Tibetan Book of the Dead*. It is very interesting. It says that souls who have passed away and are yet to be reborn love marriage processions. These disembodied beings follow the newlyweds, thinking, "Are you going to be my mommy? Are you my daddy? Can I be born in your house because I need a body to fulfill all my desires?" It is a funny description. These souls push away other disembodied souls, also vying for reincarnation, saying, "Hey they are my prospective parents, not yours. Go away, find your own marriage procession. I saw these two people first, and they are going to be my parents."

There is an urgency to take birth, and this birth is dependent upon *yathā-śrutam*, which means that the birth is in accordance with the *śāstra*. *Yathā-karma* means according to one's karma. So, according to whatever karma is there, this person is reborn.

For example, one might complain of a mind that is always wandering. In the next life, they could be born as a frog, constantly jumping and leaping, because karma has a sense of humor. It is not all cut and dry. There are many lifetimes, many experiences, and this whole thing is a charade.

Karma is a model that comes to an end as soon as you understand that you are not the doer. The doer is you, but you are not the doer. When the notion that you are the agent of action is falsified, there is no *karmaphala* that accrues to you. It is like a dead person's bank account; the person is not there. Or it is like a dream lottery that you have won, which you cannot use as a down payment for buying a house in the waking state.

That is exactly how it is. You have awakened to a new you that is neither the doer nor is done-in, by others' doings. Therefore, there is no reason for another birth. The cause of birth is self-ignorance. Once self-ignorance is taken care of, there is no more need for being born.

Question: Pardon me if I misquote, but in the Bhagavad-Gita, Krishna says, "If you are dying or at the end of your life, just think of me and I will take care of you." This is a question that my children ask. We were raised Catholic, but we all sit together and read the Bhagavad-Gita and the Bible every day; they love it. One of my daughters talked about another part of the Gita, where it is said, "They worship lowly gods, these demons, and so they go to these places."

Answer: I will explain that. It is often misunderstood. I am very happy that you are reading the Gita with your children.

Let us take the first part of the question: *antakāle ca mām eva smaran muktvā kalevaram*. Lord Krishna says that the one who gives up the body while thinking of me at the last moment achieves redemption. This is not a salvational statement as you know, but there is redemption from rebirth; that is the idea. Because even in the last minute, when you have this awareness that Krishna and I are one, Then you go to *Bhagavān*; that is the idea.

It is actually very beautiful, and Pujya Swamiji used to say that this is the reason Hindus got very clever. They thought, "Oh, that is easy! I have to think of *Bhagavān* all the time, so I will name one child Narayana and another Krishna." So, whenever they call the child Krishna, they are thinking of *Bhagavān*. They believed they had found a loophole, having the love for the child translate into love for *Bhagavān*, which is, in fact, in a way, the same thing.

Unfortunately, it does not work because of the prevalence of pet names. Krishna becomes Kittu, and Narayana becomes Nanu, so it does not quite work as intended. But jokes apart, the idea is that there is comfort in that promise. In the Bhagavad-Gita, there are certain promises. *Bhagavān* says: *na me bhaktaḥ praṇaśyati,* my devotee is never destroyed.

This is one promise. The other promise is the one you mentioned: "Even when you pray to me at the last minute, I am there for you." This is very comforting. The idea is that whatever you think of at the last minute is what you have been thinking of all the time. So, if somebody says, "Please think of Krishna at the last minute," most people will say, "Last minute only, not now. So why should I worry now?" But do we know when the last minute is? The last minute can be the next minute. We do not know that. Therefore, the idea is not to pray but to be a prayerful person.

A person who prays is someone for whom prayer is a discrete act, separate from oneself. Whereas a prayerful person is one for whom all acts are done with a prayerful attitude. So, this is the first part of your question.

The second part of the question comes from the Bhagavad-Gita, Chapter 16, *Daivāsura Sampat* is often poorly translated as "Godly and Devilish Treasures." It is more about how some people behave like *rākṣasas*. Everyone knows it as demonic in nature, characterized by selfish demands and a rank disregard for others.

Lord Krishna systematically examines their daily life. What do they eat? They eat leftovers. Like the nursery rhyme: "Some like it hot, some like it cold, some like it in the pot nine days old." If the pudding is nine days old, what *prāṇa* can it have to give you nourishment? This is called *tāmasika* food. The asuras eat old things, or things with strong odors. Their eating habits reflect their angry and resentful nature.

How do they pray? They invoke ghosts and spirits, praying to disembodied entities. If one prays to such entities for favors, they should consider asking *Bhagavān* instead, who can grant everything. This is the essence.

Some forms of worship are terrifying in nature. These are done in cremation grounds, often in the middle of the night. Sometimes, harm to others is involved because prayers for one's success is offered at the cost of others' failure. Saying, "Let me be successful," is a *sattvic* prayer, but saying, "Let this person fail," is not. People who pray this way attract similar entities.

Question: I would like you to speak on grief and the stages of grief. I recently lost my grandma and my best friend. I was happy to see my grandma go; she was 98. But my friend died quickly of cancer, and we did not

get to say goodbye. I find peace with my grandma's passing, but I cannot find peace or recover from the loss of my friend. She was only 35 years old.

Answer: I am very sorry for your loss. Losing someone unexpectedly is very difficult. Even though your friend is now free from suffering, it does not lessen the pain you feel. Grief means two things. One, there is an emptiness, a void. Nobody will be able to fill that spot. You can make a hundred more friends, but it will not be the same. Everyone here could come to you after the satsang and say they want to be your friend, and I hope they do, but still, it will not make up for the one who is missing. Why is there this gap? Why is there this loss, this feeling of emptiness? Because the friendship is now one-sided. You still relate to the person as your friend, but there is nobody there to be a friend back to you. That is why there is this gap, and it takes time to heal. Time is *Bhagavān*. Time is the best healer.

The stages of grief often refer to five or six stages, encompassing various emotions.

Grief brings denial, pain, anger, and agony, among other feelings. From the standpoint of the *śāstra*, a key aspect of grief is non-acceptance. This is not just denial in the sense of not believing the friend is gone. Rather, it is an active resistance to participating in the "friendless" reality which is left behind because it happened against one's wishes.

This non-acceptance is a significant component of grief. The first component is the daily loss, the constant missing of the person, and the inability to share moments with them. This is part one of the pain.

Part two is the inability to move on, the inability to accept what has happened. For the first part, time will heal. It also helps to keep the memory of your friend alive by doing some of the things you enjoyed together or by supporting a cause that was dear to them. Keeping the memory alive is a nice way to overcome that first component.

For the second component of grief in the form of non-acceptance, you start by accepting the non-acceptance. Can you accept the non-acceptance? If you say no, then I will ask if you can accept the non-acceptance of the non-acceptance. I will keep asking until, at some point, you have to give up and say yes, I finally accept the non-acceptance of the non-acceptance of the non-acceptance of the non-acceptance of the non-acceptance of the non-acceptance. That is the starting point.

Then every day it is one less non-acceptance because you have accepted another non-acceptance. So, give yourself the time to grieve. It is okay.

Finally, I will say grief is non-separate from *Bhagavān*. Imagine if you bottle everything up, where would it go? It would be like a pressure cooker, and you would blow your top off. That is no fun. Grief needs an outlet, a safe outlet that does not hurt yourself or anyone else. Write it out or cry it out. Surround yourself with things that comfort you and keep the memory alive; that really helps. It gives you a project.

I am glad you brought up this question today. Kudos to you for asking it in public and sharing your experience. That alone is very helpful. I hope that was helpful.

Online Teaching Resources

Question: I know you mentioned something about reading the Upanishads being a waste of time and that we need to find somebody to teach us. However, I would like to be prepared for those teachings. Do you have any specific recommendations on how to read the explanations?

Answer: It is best not read the Upanishads on your own, and instead, to listen to a teacher. You are already prepared to listen, and the listening itself is a form of preparation. The more you listen, the more the mind gets prepared.

In the olden days, gurus would send students to the cowshed, where they would take care of the cows, taking them to pasture, cleaning them, milking them, and feeding them. This sometimes lasted for 33 years. In one Upanishad, it is mentioned that Indra, the king of heaven, stayed in the guru's ashram for 105 years doing this kind of work.

However, we live in different times now, and people have an urgency and lack of time. Now, we simultaneously keep listening and preparing the mind also.

Question: I must appreciate the great mastery you have over the English language and the way you present these lectures. The first time I was exposed to Vedanta was through a lecture I attended after a hard day's work. Slowly, I wanted to learn more and more. I was able to attend a lecture by a friend on the primer text *Tattvabodha,* which gave me a lot of clarity. Where can I listen to your lectures?

Answer: Yes, that is how it begins. Once you realize the greatness of Vedanta, you naturally want more. You can join our online classes and explore our YouTube channel and podcast recordings. Additionally, there are many Gita Home Study groups available globally.

Thank you. May all be happy and healthy. May all be filled with loving kindness. May all grow in maturity and compassion.

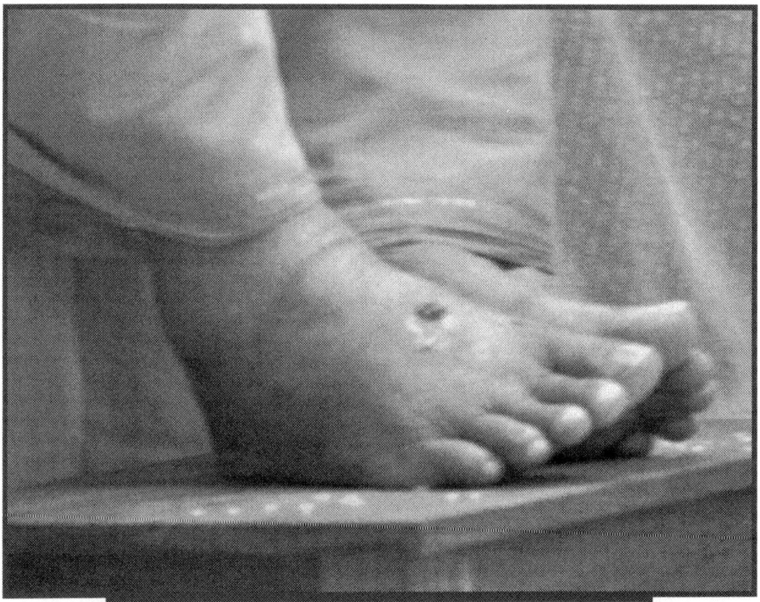

Oṁ Tat Sat

GLOSSARY

abhiśeka	Ritual bathing of deities with sacred liquids
acchedya	That which cannot be cut
adaḥ	That
adāhya	That which cannot be burned
adharma	Improper action
adhibhūta	Centered on the five elements i.e., one's surroundings
adhideva	Centered on God
adhiṣṭhāna	The truth or the source
adhyāsa	Erroneous perception
adhyātma	Centered on the self
āditya	Sun
adṛṣṭa	Invisible (referring to deferred results of karma)
advaita	Non-dual, without a second

āgāmi-karma	Karma done in this life that either immediately bears fruit or joins the karmic collection known as *sañcita*
ahaṅkāra	I-notion, ego
ahimsā	Non-violence, abstinence from harming others through thought, word, or deed
ajñāna	Ignorance
akartṛ	Non-doer
akledya	That which cannot be damaged by water
ānanda	Limitlessness, wholeness
ananta	Limitless, infinite
anātman	Not-I, objects of cognition
anirākaraṇaṃ	Non-rejection, non-denial
antaḥkaraṇa	Inner-instrument, which includes the mind, intellect, emotions, and ego
antaraṅga	Internal or inward
anubhava	Experience
anugraha	Grace
aparigraha	Non-hoarding

aparōkṣa	The self-evident self which is not removed
ārati	Waving of the camphor lamp done at the end of a *pūjā*
ārṣa	Coming from the *ṛṣis*
artha	Object, meaning, security, or purpose
asaṅga	Uninvolved
aśōṣya	That which cannot be damaged by the wind
Aṣṭāvakra	A sage with eight bends, author of the *Aṣṭāvakra Gītā*
asura	The one who revels in the sense objects by going against dharma
atat	Not that, opposite of *tat*
ātatāyin	A terrorist
Atharvaveda	The name of a Veda
ātmajña	One who knows the *ātman*
ātmajñāna	Self-knowledge
ātman	The I, the self
avadhūta	A liberated sage

Avadhūta-Gītā	A sacred text attributed to Dattatreya that expounds the nature of the self
avatāra	*Īśvara* manifesting on the Earth in a certain form
avidyā	Ignorance
bahiraṅga	External, outward
bhadra	Auspicious
bhaga	Six virtues: overlordship, wealth, knowledge, dispassion, strength, and power
Bhagavān	One endowed with the *bhagas*
Bhagavat-prasāda	An attitude of receiving the results of action as a gift from *Bhagavān*
bhajan (Hindi)	Devotional chants and music
bhakta	A devotee
bhakti	Devotion
bhāṣya	A traditional commentary on a primary work such as the Upanishad which explains the words of the Upanishad and explains itself
bhava	Existence, and a word that is also used for *saṃsāra*

bhikṣā	Alms
bhoktṛ	Experiencer
Brahmā	Lord *Brahmāji*, the creator
brahmacārin	A student of the Veda
brahmajñāna	Knowledge of Brahman
Brahman	That which is limitlessly big, the truth of the self
brāhmaṇa	The one who is qualified to know Brahman
brahmaniṣṭha	One established in knowledge of Brahman
Brahmasūtra	An analytical text of aphorisms composed by Vyāsa
brahmavidyā	Knowledge of Brahman
buddhi	Intellect
cakra	A wheel. Generally used in relation to *saṃsāra* as in "the wheel of *saṃsāra*."
citta	The faculty of emotions
cittanaiścalya	Steadfastness of the mind, gained through meditation
cittaśuddhi	Purification of the mind by neutralizing strong likes and dislikes

dehin	Indweller of the body
deva	A god or deity
devatā	A deity
dharma	A universal matrix of norms
dhyāna	Meditation
digdevatā	The deities of the presiding directions
dṛg	Seer
dṛṣṭa	Seen
dṛṣṭaphala	Immediate results of karma
dṛśya	Object of sight
duḥkha	Sorrow
dveṣa	Strong prejudices
ekādaśī	Eleventh day of the lunar fortnight, namely the eleventh day after either the new or full Moon
Godāvari	A sacred river in India
grantha	Manuscript
gṛhastha	A householder
gu	Ignorance
guṇa	Attribute, quality

guru	Remover of self-ignorance, teacher of *ātmavidyā*
gurukula	A place of Vedic study where one lives and studies with the teacher
Gurupūrṇimā	The birthday of *Bhagavān* Vyāsa, a day dedicated to celebrating Gurus
homā	A Vedic fire ritual in which oblations are offered
hṛṣīkeṣaḥ	Lord of all the senses, Krishna, a name for Lord Krishna
idam	This, referring to something that can be objectified
iṣṭadevatā	One's favorite form of the Lord
Īśāvāsya	A name of an Upanishad
Īśvara	The cause of the universe, the overlord of the creation
Īśvarārpaṇa-buddhi	An attitude of dedicating all actions to *Īśvara*
Īśvaratva	*Īśvara*-hood
jagat	The entire universe starting with one's body-mind-sense complex
jagatkāraṇa	The cause of the universe, *Īśvara*
japa	Mental repetition of a mantra

jīva	A sentient form of Brahman, identified with the physical body
jīvatva	*Jīva*-hood, the status of identifying as an individual
jñāna	Knowledge
jñānin	The knower of Brahman, a wise person
jyotiṣa	Astrology
kāla	Time
kalaśa	A sacred water-pot used for rituals
kāma	Desire
karma	Action, also used to refer to consequences of action
karmaphala	Fruit of action
karmaphaladātṛ	*Īśvara* as the giver of the fruits of action
karmayoga	A life devoted to preparing for self- knowledge by dedicating one's actions to *Īśvara* as a means for self-growth
kartṛ	The doer
kartṛtva	Doer-ship, identifying as the agent of action

karuṇā	Compassion
Kāśī	An ancient name for Varanasi, a sacred city in India
Kaunteya	Son of Kunti, another name for Arjuna
kāyika	Physical
krodha	Anger
kṣānti	Accommodation
loka	World or realm
manas	Mind
mantra	A chant
mithyā	A name given to the empirical reality which depends on Brahman for its existence
modaka	A sweet dish stuffed with jaggery and coconut
mokṣa	Liberation from a sense of bondage
mukti	Liberation
mumukṣu	One desirous of liberation
mumukṣutva	The state of desiring *mokṣa*
namaḥ	Salutation, surrender to what is

namaskāra	Enactment of salutations, in the form of a bow
Narmada	A holy river in India
neti-neti	A method of teaching used to negate changing attributes to reveal the changeless self
nididhyāsana	Contemplation
nimitta	A cause or an instrumental
Nirvāṇaṣaṭkam	A six-verse composition on Vedanta attributed to Adi Shankara
niṣṭhā	A committed lifestyle
nitya	Eternal, not subject to time
Oṁ	Sacred sound that refers to Brahman as consciousness and as *Īśvara* the cause of the universe
Pañcadaśī	A highly regarded Vedantic text by Swami Vidyaranya
Pañcatantra	An ancient collection of fables and moral stories
pāpa	Uncomfortable situations as a result of actions not in congruence with dharma in this or other lives

pāramārthika	The absolute reality where there is nothing other than Brahman, the self
parameśvara	The Lord, *Īśvara,* the Creator
paramparā	Lineage
prakaraṇa-grantha	A text on Vedanta which systematically unfolds the vision of oneness
pralaya	Dissolution, resolution of the universe
pramāṇa	Means of knowledge
pramātr	The knower
prāṇa	Life force
prārabdha	The karma to be exhausted in the course of one lifetime
prasāda	Gift from *Bhagavān*
prātibhāsika	Subjective reality
pratipakṣa-bhāvana	Taking the opposite stance
pratyagātman	Inner-self
pūjā	Ritualistic worship at an altar or temple

puṇya	Comfortable situations as a result of dharmic actions in this and other lives
purāṇa	Ancient mythological texts authored by Vyāsa
pūrṇa	Full, whole
pūruṣa	The indweller of the citadel, called the body, *jivā* and the one that fills up everything, *Īśvara*
puruṣārtha	That which is desired by all human beings, the fourfold goals of life: dharma (righteouness) *artha* (security), *kāma* (pleasure), *mokṣa* (liberation)
rāga	Strong preferences
rajas	The principle of motion and restlessness, the name of a *guṇa*
rākṣasa	A person who goes against *dharma* in pursuit of wealth, power, position
rasa	Essence, longing
Ṛgveda	A name of a Veda
ṛṣi	Sage
ru	Remover
Rudram	A Vedic prayer

saccidānanda	Limitless existence and awareness resting in a conscious being, definition of *ātman*
sādhaka	A spiritual aspirant
sādhana	Means of accomplishment, practice
sādhu	A mendicant
sādhya	To be accomplished
saguṇa	Having attributes or qualities
sākṣin	Witness
sama	Equal
samādhana	Mental focus, one pointedness
samādhi	Absorption without subject-object division in meditation
sāmānya	Universal
samaṣṭi	Total
samatva	Equanimity
Sāmaveda	The name of a *Veda*
saṃsāra	A life of becoming
saṃskāra	Past impressions
saṃskṛtabuddhi	One whose intellect is refined through spiritual discipline

saṃvāda	Teacher-student dialogue
sanātana	Everlasting
sañcita	The store house of accumulated karma, the cause of countless rebirths
saṅga	Involvement, dysfunctional connection
saṅkalpa	Intention
sannyāsa	Renunciation, monasticism
sannyāsin	A renunciant
śānti	Peace
Saraswati	A sacred river in ancient India, the Goddess of knowledge and music
sarvagata	All-pervasive; present everywhere
sarvātmabhāva	The vision of the self as everything
sarvātman	The self of all beings
śāstra	Teachings, sacred texts
sat	Limitless existence
satsaṅga	The company of people interested in *sat*

sattva	Godliness, the name of a *guṇa*
satya	Same as *sat*
Śaunaka	An ancient sage
sevā	Service
siddha	Evident
śīrṣāsana	Headstand
śiṣya	One worthy of being taught
śiva	Auspicious
śivaliṅga	An oval stone representing Lord Shiva
śloka	A hymn of praise
śraddhā	Trust pending understanding in the *pramāṇa* and the guru
śravaṇa	Listening to Vedanta from a teacher
śrotriya	One who has studied from a teacher belonging to a lineage
sṛṣṭi	Creation
śruti	Primary texts i.e. Vedas and Upanishads
sthāne	In place
sthāṇu	Unmoving, steady

sthira	Steadfast
sthiti	Sustenance of creation
stotra	A hymn of praise
śuddhi	Purity
svāḥā	An expression
svarūpa	Essential nature
svarūpalakṣaṇa	A definition that unfolds the essential nature of Brahman
svataḥ-siddha	Self-evident
tamas	Ignorance, sorrow, the name of a *guṇa*
tapas	Spiritual austerities
tat	That, referring to the cause of the universe
taṭasthalakṣaṇa	A definition that unfolds the incidental nature of Brahman as the cause of the universe
Tattvabodha	The name of a Vedantic text attributed to Adi Shankara
titikṣā	Cheerful forbearance
tvam	You
upadeśa	Teaching, instruction

upādhi	That which remaining near an object imparts its attributes to that object. For example: *upādhi* of a red flower near a crystal makes the it appear red.
Upanishad	Revealed texts appearing at the end of the Vedas which unfold the nature of the self as limitlessly whole
vairāgya	Dispassion, objectivity
vaiśvānara	The Lord in the form of the digestive fire
vākśuddhi	Purification of speech
vāktapas	Discipline with regard to speech
vastu	Reality
Vedas	Revealed knowledge
vedāṅga	Auxiliary texts connected to the Veda
vega	Pressure
vidvān	A wise person
vidyā	Knowledge
vijñāna	Well ascertained knowledge
viṣaya	Object

viveka	Discrimination between the infinite and the finite
Vivekacūḍāmaṇi	A Vedantic text attributed to Adi Shankara
vyavahāra	Transaction
vyavahārika	Empirically reality
yajña	A fire ritual
Yamuna	A sacred river in India
yati	A spiritual aspirant
yoga	A means for accomplishing something, a way of life
yogin	A sincere, practitioner of yoga
yuktaḥ	Endowed with, united with

ओँ सर्वे जनाः सुखिनो भवन्तु
सर्वं ब्रह्मार्पणमस्तु। शुभमस्तु॥

Made in the USA
Las Vegas, NV
01 October 2024

96058531R00229